THE
BUY-IN
THEORY

THE SIMPLE IDEA THAT
CHANGES EVERYTHING

MATT
ELLEDGE

Published by SOK Enterprise, LLC
Copyright 2017 © Matthew Elledge

Digital ISBN: 978-0-9989897-0-9
Paperback ISBN: 978-0-9989897-1-6

Interior Design: Christina Culbertson, 3CsBooks.com

DEDICATION

It is with the most sincere gratitude that I dedicate
this book to the men, women and families of
the United States Armed Forces:

You are this nation's finest treasure and the true
embodiment of everything this book represents.

CONTENTS

BUY-IN: A SOLDIER'S STORY

The strength of our Nation is our Army. The strength of our Army is our Soldiers and the strength of our Soldiers is our Families. That's what makes us Army Strong.

—GEN ODIERNO

The United States Army is an extraordinary institution. Formed in 1775 from small bands of militiamen to fight for independence from Britain, today it has nearly 990,000 Active Duty, National Guard and Reserve members based in more than 70 countries with missions ranging from peacekeeping efforts and humanitarian relief to security and law enforcement, and, yes, the dirty business of war. The Army functions as one unit, but look closer, and you will find within that structure are individuals from all walks of life, with different values, different cultures, different languages, and different motivations, who all make the free choice to enlist and serve. How can such a body so constituted and so diverse move and act as one to accomplish all these missions? In short, it is buy-in.

Buy-in is a concept that is hard to nail down, but at its core, is the *commitment to something greater than ourselves* that makes us available for heroic and creative efforts, even at great risk to our own safety. It's the willingness to make sacrifices (large and small) for the benefit of the team because we know we are an important part of something bigger than ourselves, that others depend on us, and that the organization's mission aligns with our own. Buy-in is what we experience when our work stops being just a *J.O.B.* and becomes, instead, a profession.

I know of what I speak because I spent 25 plus years in my true profession: following and leading men and women in the US Army, in tasks varying from filing accounting paperwork to fighting insurgents on the front lines in Baghdad. I observed the workings of buy-in throughout my career, both in and out of combat, from my very first posting. I learned to inspire soldiers who were under my command and care, and I have come to apply the principles of buy-in to my civilian life as the director of the Texas Veterans Land Board, a Texas State agency devoted to serving Veterans.

But why should the concept of buy-in—something I learned in the military—be of interest to you? After all, the army is different from corporations, small businesses, or nonprofit organizations in some very fundamental ways. Soldiers must take orders from their superiors or risk punishment. They cannot simply quit their jobs. You may think it makes sense that the army can accomplish extraordinary things because the leadership has leverage over the members of their organization in a way that businesses do not. You might conclude that buy-in wouldn't work in your organization.

I disagree. I believe that buy-in is an essential component in a collection of qualities that makes *any* organization—military, commercial, or nonprofit—more effective. Buy-in grew organically within the army because of the nature of its missions. Heroic efforts aren't simply nice to have. They are critical. To get so many different people pulling in the same direction during extremely difficult circumstances requires buy-in. Leaders command, but it is a volunteer army; members are not drafted, and leaders do not have the power to force their commitment. In circumstances where there is no love or respect for their leaders, soldiers will not give their all for the mission and won't make sacrifices for the good of others. When the organization is infused with buy-in, however, soldiers are willing to make the ultimate sacrifice. Let me show you what I mean with an example.

A young soldier, let's call him Private Jenson, showed up at his unit from boot camp. The other soldiers within the unit had just completed a train-up, including live-fire exercises and physical training, to prepare for deployment to Operation Iraqi Freedom. The members of the unit had prepared, knew how to work together, and were ready: they had become a band of brothers. It's not easy to join a group that's already established, but the leadership within the unit, including Sergeant Reilly, took their new soldier under their collective wing.

The leadership knew Jenson was coming, and although they didn't like it because he would miss the train-up for their mission, they set to work getting him up to speed so they could build a cohesive unit before deployment. They assigned Jenson a sponsor who contacted him long before he arrived to welcome him, open a dialog, and ensure he had everything he needed to integrate quickly. When Jenson arrived, they taught him the history of the unit and trained him in the tactics and techniques used in combat to get him working in tandem with other members of the unit.

Once Reilly and the rest of the leadership felt he was ready, they openly recognized him for his accomplishments in front of the unit, and the soldiers accepted him as a part of their band of brothers because they had gone through the same integration process. He was one of them.

The unit deployed to Iraq, and shortly thereafter, they come in direct contact with the enemy in a firefight. Everyone knew what to do, including our young soldier. During the fight, Reilly was shot and severely wounded. Jenson knew he needed to get him to a medic as quickly as possible. While under fire, he moved toward Reilly while his unit continued to engage with the enemy. During his dash to retrieve his sergeant, Jenson was shot in the leg. Undaunted, he continued to make his way to Reilly.

The rest of the unit began to turn the tide on the enemy, but just as he reached Reilly, Jenson was shot again, this time in the arm. Despite his injuries, our young soldier started first aid on Reilly while his unit finally took control of the situation and cleared the area of enemy combatants. Because he had lost a lot of blood, Jenson passed out as his buddies arrived. They worked quickly to render first aid and evacuate both injured men to the nearest aid station. When Jenson woke up, he saw his command sergeant major, the senior enlisted soldier of the unit, standing over him. Without a thought to his own life-threatening injuries, Jenson asked about his unit leader. Thanks to the young soldier's efforts—and those of the rest of the unit—Reilly survived, and Jenson also went on to recover from his injuries.

Jenson was committed to his band of brothers and their mission. He put himself in danger to protect a man he had only recently met. Even after being injured, his first concern was for the life of someone else. What made his last-minute, potentially disastrous addition to this unit a success? Jenson had buy-in. His boot camp training had established a level of commitment in him that meant, by the time he was assigned to his unit, he was already committed to its success. The way the unit leadership welcomed him continued to build on that solid foundation.

Just as buy-in was a prerequisite for Jenson's successful integration into his new unit, it is also a prerequisite for a successful business. Without a commitment from your leaders, managers, and employees, your organization cannot reach its full potential. Now, outside of the military, most organizations do not ask their members to risk their lives during their daily duties. But the techniques that create this level of buy-in in the military will help you create the level of commitment your organization needs to grow, thrive, and even exceed your goals.

All this leads to the question: *how* does the army get a group of young men and women who have different values and come from different cultures, religions, and upbringings?

How does it bring them to the point where they're willing to put their life on the line for the others? Just as important: how do we replicate that in business? That's what we'll explore in this book.

In the pages that follow, I lay out four principles that will lead to an environment of buy-in within your business or organization. We'll discuss the importance of trust, a clear vision, good communication, and effective leadership—and how to develop these traits in your yourself and your people.

This will be particularly relevant if you are a leader of a small project, starting your own business that is beginning to grow, or the CEO of a large company. If you are losing good employees and can't figure out why this book is for you. Have you ever stopped and wondered what this loss in personnel costs you in recruiting and training new employees? Could that money be better spent elsewhere?

The four areas we explore will help you gain and retain a quality workforce—the right team for the long term to help your business prosper. If you need more time to spend with family and friends, to enjoy what life is all about, this book can help you create an environment that will allow for that. If you need time away from the daily grind to focus on big picture planning, the same methods will help you create momentum in your business, so decisions are made better and faster, customer service improves, and sales and marketing become more effective. Your employees will feel empowered to make your business better and you will get your time back.

These are big promises, but after 25 years in the army—an organization that takes people from all walks of life and builds them into teams able to fight and win our nation's wars, support humanitarian missions, and keep the peace in turbulent times—I know that buy-in is key to the success of any business or organization.

I spent the last three years of my military career taking notes on how the army creates the type of buy-in needed to face down and win against an enemy that wants to destroy us and our way of life. I use those some principles now to lead my new organization, and we are succeeding together as a team. If you follow the same principles, which are outlined in this book, you and your organization will soon reap the benefits of buy-in.

Read these chapters, implement the actions recommended, and go to www.embracetheedge.com for more information, tips, techniques, and inspiration for you and your business or organization.

2

INTRODUCTION

In any moment of decision, the best thing to do is make the right decision, the second best is to make the wrong decision, and the worst thing you can do is nothing.

—THEODORE ROOSEVELT

Before we dive into the principles of creating buy-in, I should tell you a little about myself. I have had the honor to serve and the privilege to lead in the United States Army for over 25 years as an infantryman. I have worked in command positions from second Lieutenant, guiding a platoon of 34 young men into combat, to Colonel and Garrison Commander, leading over 5,000 of the most patriotic people I have ever met (our Department of the Army civilians) on Fort Hood Texas, which was one of the largest Army Installations in North America. Now retired from the military, I have the honor of continuing to serve those who have served our nation: our veterans. More specifically, I work as the Director of the Texas Veterans Land Board.

During my career, I have deployed on multiple combat tours and a humanitarian mission and served in various staff and command positions along the way. I have also had the incredible opportunity to be educated by some of the greatest strategists and tacticians of our time. Most of those names you will never have heard of (and some you will), but all are talented leaders who continue to stand between our way of life and those that would destroy it.

Not only have I been educated by the best, but I have led and been led by some of the most talented men and women the United States has to offer. They are truly national treasures and wonderful representatives of all that is great about our nation.

As in any organization, the army does have a few bad leaders, and in my 25 years of service, I watched some of them struggle. Thankfully, they were very few and far between and were usually culled from the herd, eventually being asked to serve the army in another capacity or, in the worst cases, ordered to leave altogether.

I know I haven't been perfect as a leader (far from it), and I have, quite frankly, been very lucky. I have had great sergeants who, with little guidance, helped turn my vision into reality, and I have served under talented officers who allowed me to fail then picked me up, taught and mentored me, and helped get me back into the fight. Those officers invested a lot of time and effort to train me.

When you think of training in the military, you might think of battle drills repeated ad nauseam. The army certainly has those along with tactics, techniques, and procedures (TTP's) that we rehearse again and again until they are ingrained in our very nature. We train on these TTPs and battle drills so often that they become a muscle reflex, and I can honestly say this training has saved my life and the lives of many other soldiers in combat.

But while battle drills and TTPs are going on, there is another type of training that the army invests heavily in, and that is the development of its leaders. They spend a lot of time and money teaching leaders to act morally and ethically, so they, in turn can train their soldiers to be the best in the world.

There is an art to training strong, moral, and effective leaders, and that is something that has fascinated me for the past 25 years. Ever since joining the army, the human dynamics involved in leadership, and the way soldiers are trained to lead from day one, has captivated me. I was intrigued to learn that the army doesn't teach its leaders *what* to think. That would fail because different soldiers or units have different goals and priorities. The ebb and flow of how soldiers and leaders communicate and relate to one another and the many situations they encounter requires the army teach its leaders *how* to think.

With proper training in how to think, those leaders are then able to adapt to the ever-changing battlefield environment, so they can quickly define problems, develop plans, and motivate soldiers to execute those plans willingly and with total confidence that the mission will be a success. Their ability to do this well is incredibly powerful.

It's even more remarkable when you consider that a leader's ability to motivate his soldiers is affected by the fact that what drives one person doesn't necessarily drive another. In a small organization, a leader could motivate all his soldiers directly. To do this, he must understand what inspires each soldier in the unit. However, when a leader is placed in a position of higher responsibility, amid larger organizations, he must motivate subordinate leaders, who then motivate their subordinate leaders, and so on.

When all this is done well, by leaders who lead—not manage (we'll get into this shortly)—there is nothing more powerful on the face of the Earth. That is why our army is the most feared land force in the world and respected by those whom we defend.

While serving in the Army, I was taught how to think about leadership and how to create an environment of commitment to something larger than ourselves. I call it the buy-in theory.

3

BUY-IN:
WHAT IS IT?

Believe you can and you're halfway there.
—THEODORE ROOSEVELT

*The best and most beautiful things in the world cannot
be seen or even touched. They must be felt with the heart.*
—HELEN KELLER

I n the military, a soldier, or any service member for that matter, is willing to lay down his life for his buddies, his leaders, his organization, and his country. That is buy-in. It is the recognition that you are a part of something larger than yourself. Those who don't have buy-in think of themselves as just another cog in the machine, but others know they are an important part of that machine. They understand that people depend on them to get their mission done, and they are determined to fulfill their responsibilities.

That is a nice concept, but what does it actually look like in an organization outside of the military? At a conference, some years ago, I posed this question to a group of very talented CEOs. I asked if a soldier is willing to lay down his life for his buddies, his leaders, and his organization, why can't we have that kind of commitment within the corporate world? Can we instill that kind of commitment in an environment where the stakes are not life or death?

The CEOs struggled with this. They had seen this kind of commitment in the private sector and assumed it was a coincidence. They had never considered it to be a culture you could deliberately create, and so had never asked *how* they could foster this environment in their own organizations. As the conference went on, we worked as a group to lay out ideas that could create buy-in within their organizations. Of course, I had to foster buy-in with them, to help them understand that the effort was worth it.

Once we started to break the concept down, they came up with ways to help each of their employees feel like an important part of the organization and become engaged in making the company better from day one. They thought of ideas to help team members understand the company's mission and how important each person is to that mission. In the end, we boiled it down to four steps to create buy-in within their organizations:

1. Building trust
2. Developing a clear vision
3. Communicating well
4. Leading effectively

If we focus on these four steps, we will have organizations in which employees trust their leaders, managers, and colleagues. The company will have a clear vision and mission that makes all its employees feel they are an important part of its future. Open and transparent communication between the team will make everyone feel that they have a say in the organization. Leaders will not try to be something they can't be but will be authentic and humbled by the privilege of leading their organization. These are the necessary ingredients for buy-in.

It is important to build this environment because it will yield a learning organization, a place that is self-correcting and adapts quickly to changes with little to no guidance from the leadership. People within the organization will believe they are part of a profession instead of just having a *J.O.B.* They will make decisions on their own to further the mission because they feel empowered to do so. As a leader, you will feel confident your workforce will do the right thing, even when you are not looking.

LEADERS AND MANAGERS

Before we move forward, I need to define whether you are a true leader or a manager. Both are important to an organization, but they serve different functions. The steps in this book will be easy to implement if you are leading, not managing. If you are clear on the difference, you will be able to see when you are behaving like a manager and address it, allowing you to move your organization forward as a leader. So, what are the differences?

Leaders have to be able to look above the fray of day-to-day activities. They must think of and develop ways to adapt to the ever-changing environment of business. Managers allow them to do that. Managers focus on the day-to-day activities and make sure the team is doing things right, so the business runs efficiently and effectively.

Leaders focus on making sure their organization is doing the right things. Leaders develop their organization's environment and get the company moving toward a clear vision, while managers maintain what the leader creates. Managers focus on systems, processes, and structures, while leaders focus on setting the managers and their subordinates up for success. Leaders ask, "*What* do we do and *why* do we do it?" Managers ask, "*How* do we do it and *when* do we need to get it done?" Lastly, leaders focus on the horizon, while managers focus on the bottom-line.

Which are you, a leader or a manager? If you spend most of your time managing when you know you should be leading, I suggest you start with letting go. This is the hard—but essential—part for any leader. To focus on creating an environment of buy-in in your organization, you need to let go of the day-to-day activities that take up much of your time. You need to trust your subordinates to execute the mission the way they see fit. So long as they meet the mission in a moral and ethical way, let them find their own way, and good on 'em.

I will talk more about trust in the next chapter. If you struggle with letting go, the guidance you find there will be of help.

A great leader and one who exemplified letting go of management so he could lead, was my Corps commander, a man who led almost half the forces of the army. While sharing his leadership philosophy to his team, he said, "There are only two kinds of soldiers in the army: the leader and the future leader." This is an attitude that works in the business world as well. While you want to distinguish between managers and leaders (as we did above), this attitude will encourage your organization to teach, coach, and mentor every member. You will grow your own leaders within the company.

Mentoring young future leaders will allow them to build their business muscle memory. They will sharpen their reflexes, grow their skills, and learn to accomplish tasks without requiring your constant guidance. When coached well, subordinates will come to you willingly with status updates and plans for the way forward. The momentum of operations will pick up, and tasks will be completed without your needing to ask. It is a wonderful thing. This is where leadership really becomes fun. I get giddy just thinking about it.

When future leaders work like this, it frees you, the leader, to think deep, look deep, and set the framework for the organization's success. It allows you to focus on improving the environment and strengthening the commitment of the employees to the organization and its mission. You can fully develop buy-in within your organization, and that will give you the foundation to go outside and sell the company, sell the product, and sell the people. It allows you to *lead* and not manage.

BECAUSE I SAID SO

For all this talk of empowering employees as future leaders, we must be honest here. Sometimes you—the current leader—must go with a "because I said so" situation. I am sure if you have led others before, you will recognize this scenario. It happens most often when you have no time to coach your subordinates through the present circumstances or when the environment makes it impossible. You find yourself giving orders without using the moment to teach your future leader. If they ask why, you tell them, "because I said so."

An example of this comes from my time as a platoon leader when we were deployed to Operations Desert Shield and Desert Storm. We had been living out in the extreme conditions of the desert (who knew the desert could be so cold?) for almost five months. It was the morning of the attack into Kuwait to destroy Iraqi forces and liberate the country, and we were trained and ready.

My company's first sergeant came driving up to me. He said, "Sir, I want you to meet your newest soldier. He just came to us last night, and the company commander wanted me to hand him off to you."

With that, the first sergeant was gone, and the soldier and I were left standing there, less than an hour from crossing the border, me with a million other things on my mind, and he, I am sure, scared out of his mind. With all the noise of equipment and artillery going off around us, I yelled to the soldier to follow me. I did the only thing I could think of at the time. I walked him over to meet his new squad leader. Now, as I tried to give the new soldier our mission and how he fit into the platoon, I knew he wasn't really listening, but I also knew his squad leader would take care of that. When I showed up at the squad leader's position with our newest soldier, he gave me the look I am sure I gave to the first sergeant. It was a look that said, "What the ...? Are you serious? Right now?" I told the soldier to do exactly what the squad leader said and he would be fine. I don't think I said the words "because I told you so," but the implication was clear.

Now, what happened after this because-I-told-you-so situation? I discovered that the soldier had done exactly what I asked him to do (which was to follow the orders of his squad leader), and he was later awarded a Silver Star for gallantry in action under enemy fire to clear out an enemy position. After combat operations ceased, I did a proper introduction and welcomed him to the platoon. I was sure that the entire squad had made him feel a part of the unit, and that the squad leader had circled back for me and explained (once the environment was safe and there was time) why he had received the orders he had from me.

I tell you this story to demonstrate that there may be moments when it is not practical to coach your future leader through the options available. If you get into this situation, it's okay. It is going to happen. Remember though, as the leader, you must circle back and explain the "*why* I said so" at some point. Nothing is more frustrating or more stymieing than a leader that lives by the "because I said so" motto and doesn't explain why later. Eventually, the subordinates are going to mutiny against the leader, the organization, and the mission. People will start coming to work because they have to and not because they want to. For them, it will become a *J.O.B.* and not a profession.

LIVER AND ONIONS

If you are a parent, I am sure you have used "because I said so." Even as a child, I am sure you heard this. I know I did—a lot. Do you remember how it made you feel when you were told to complete a task with no apparent purpose? You know as well as I do how you reacted when you were given the "because I said so" speech. You would eventually do what you were asked, but you weren't happy about it, and you probably let your parents know that. Oh, and I am sure you (like me) put in the least amount of effort you could get away with.

When I was a child, my dad loved liver and onions. I didn't and would do anything not to eat them. Now, I grew up as a military brat of a noncommissioned officer, so money was always tight, and I would get the "kids are starving in China" speech when I refused to eat my liver and onions. I was willing to pay for the postage to mail it to those kids just so I wouldn't have to eat the meal. It didn't matter. My mom would stay on me to eat that liver. I tried everything to avoid it. I even ate a whole bowl of green beans, of which I wasn't a fan, to avoid eating the liver and onions.

When my mom had had enough, I would get the because-I told-you-so speech. I received no backup from my dad, so I would sit at the dinner table and play with my food, and after what seemed like hours, I would eat the liver and onions. You would think, from the fuss I'd made, that my mom was forcing me to eat poison (yes, I do have a dramatic side). Sometimes I would wear my mom out, like when she had to go do something else, but usually, she would sit there for as long as she could and "manage" me to ensure I ate the liver and onions.

As a child, no one ever explained to me that I had to eat liver and onions because it was what my parents could afford and I needed the nutrients. Instead of explaining the "why I said so," my mom chose to manage the situation by sitting at the dinner table, watching over me, and getting more and more frustrated. She spent a lot of time on this, and it did not improve our relationship or my behavior.

My point here is if you are managing a project, mission or organization when you should be leading, and saying "because I said so" without explaining why, you are wasting your time, weakening your relationships, and discouraging your employees from performing well. You are also missing out on opportunities to gain new perspectives and solutions. When you lead, not manage, and explain why you do things, your employees have the chance to suggest ways of doing the task, project, or mission better the next time. You never know … maybe a team member knows how to make liver and onions taste better.

TAKE ACTION

1. Understand the concept of buy-in.

Buy-in is when people are committed to something larger than themselves. They are committed to the organization, their leaders, and their teammates. They believe and take ownership of what they are doing and want to be a part of making the mission and organization successful. When your organization has buy-in, you as a leader can focus on the future and setting the right environment for your team, and your team can focus on the organization and the day-to-day operations.

2. Know why your organization needs buy-in.

Because I said so. Just kidding. When you have buy-in from your organization, you get your time back and that allows you to focus on the big picture. You can look out, think deep, and form a clear vision for the way ahead. You build leaders within the organization. The momentum of the organization can increase exponentially because its future leaders are making decisions and executing operations with minimal guidance from you as their leader. They know what needs to get done, and they ensure it happens.

3. Assess your organization for buy-in.

If you, the leader, are watching over your people "eating liver and onions," then you are managing them, and you don't have buy-in. If your people are coming to you with a "new sauce" to enjoy "eating liver and onions" then you have buy-in. If you are getting overwhelmed with day to day decisions then you don't have buy-in. If your people are coming to you with solutions rather than problems because they feel empowered to do so, then you have buy-in.

So now that you understand what buy-in is, why you need it, and how to tell if you have it, the next question is *how* do you build it into your organization?

4

STEP ONE: TRUST

Trust is the highest form of human motivation.
It brings out the very best in people.

—STEPHEN COVEY

We all know the importance of trust in our personal relationships. I trust my wife will take care of our home while I am away, I trust my children will be there for me in my old age, and I trust my dog will come back after he chases a squirrel. Trust is essential to these relationships. It is the confidence we have in others, and a belief in their abilities, strengths, and consistency.

Trust is also essential to any organization. It is the foundation for everything an organization must do to be successful. For team members to do their best work, they must have confidence in their colleagues, their leadership, and their organization. They must believe in what they are doing.

As with personal relationships, trust in business must be earned and then it must be continuously nurtured. There are three areas in which to gain and maintain trust in business. These "trust pillars" include the following:

1. **Trust in the organization.** The employee and leaders must trust that the organization has their best interests in mind.

2. **Trust in the employee from the leadership.** The leadership must have confidence in the employees to do what is best for the organization.

3. **Trust in the leaders from the employees.** The employees must be assured that the leadership has their best interests at heart and is going to train them and empower them to be engaged in the success of the company.

TRUST IN THE ORGANIZATION: SPONSORSHIP

Organizations can gain the trust of their employees and leaders in several ways, but the most effective method I have seen is the Army's Sponsorship Program. Sponsorship is a structured way of welcoming new recruits, training and educating them and integrating them into your organization.

Through this process, the organization shows that it is trustworthy. It is a method that works incredibly well and can be implemented in any organization.

In the Army, soldiers frequently move from post to post. With each transfer, the new unit must earn the soldier's trust quickly, so they can be ready for any mission. In your organization, you must also earn the trust of new employees quickly, so they can contribute to their projects and the overall mission more quickly.

This transition is not easy for a new employee, or newly transferred soldier. As I mentioned earlier, growing up, I was a military brat and we moved countless times, all over the world, so I saw and felt firsthand how stressful these transitions can be for a soldier and their family. Unfortunately, during the time my dad served in the military, there wasn't much of an official sponsorship program. Informally my father had friends, or friends of friends, serving at the new unit, and they would help us get settled. When I entered the service in the early 90's, it was a little better, but nothing like the Army's current sponsorship program.

Today, the Army spends an extraordinary amount of energy and resources on quickly integrating and building trust within the units across the Army. The sponsorship program is the key to gaining that trust. It works like this:

When the army prepares to change a soldier's duty station, the current and future units contact one another, and a sponsor is assigned to the transitioning soldier in the new unit. The sponsor reaches out to the transferring soldier and welcomes him or her to the unit. They provide information in advance of the transfer, and once the new soldier arrives on base, they welcome them in person and help with administrative and social integration for the soldier and their family.

In the past, this didn't happen. You were given orders and 30 days later you showed up at your next assignment. Now the army is much better at identifying soldiers who will change stations in six months to a year. That's a good thing and now that it's easier to communicate with email, cell phones, and social media, sponsors and soldiers can begin to get to know one another immediately.

When I was a battalion commander leading about 1,000 soldiers, my personnel officer (think human resources) and my command sergeant major (CSM), the senior enlisted soldier in the unit, would sit down with me every month, and update me on who we were receiving and when. As soon as we found out, I would send a letter via snail mail to the incoming soldier welcoming them to the unit. Along with the letter, I included brochures about the post and the area, the unit history, and the name and contact information of their sponsor. At the same time, the sponsor would also reach out to the incoming soldier.

We did our best to link up a soldier of about the same age, rank, and marital status. A sponsor who was single and lived in the barracks wasn't much use to an incoming soldier who was married with two kids. While the sponsor would contact the soldier the spouses from the battalion would contact the incoming spouse, to welcome them to the unit and the area, and let them both know that they were available to answer any questions and provide the "inside" information. It wasn't perfect, but it worked, and the hope was to make the soldier and family feel welcome and integrate them into the unit quickly. It was the first step in gaining the soldier's trust.

Once the soldier arrived at the unit, the sponsor would link up with the soldier and help him settle in. Along with the administrative requirements of making sure new soldiers were getting paid, had housing, had all their equipment, and so on, the sponsor would also begin to train the soldier on the history of the unit and make sure they were assigned and qualified for the appropriate weapon. The new soldier would receive a physical fitness test and learn the basic battle drills within our unit. Once complete, the soldier would go before a board and be tested on their knowledge of the unit and the basics of being a soldier. Once they passed, they were formally welcomed to the unit by me and the CSM. There was no hazing involved. We just wanted to make sure the soldier was ready to deploy, fight, and win when called.

While the soldier was being integrated, we would further build on the trust we had gained from our sponsorship program by working with the soldier's family. Our Family Readiness Group, all volunteers and led by the spouses, would welcome the spouse and provide support when needed. This support could range from something as simple as providing a gift basket of items that we all need when we move from one place to another, to providing transport to the different agencies on post, or even providing language translation if required. For our young single soldiers, we would write a note or even make a phone call to let their parents know the soldier had arrived, and update them on how they were doing. This was very powerful. I learned to do this, because every now and again, I would get a call from a parent asking if their son or daughter was okay. It is amazing how a simple letter, email, or phone call can mean so much to the mothers and fathers of these national treasures, our soldiers.

Our great Family Readiness Group was born from the many deployments the unit had completed in the past. There is a saying in the army: "You enlist a soldier, but you retain a family." The thought was that, if the family was taken care of, then the soldier could focus on his mission because he knew there was a support group for the family. When it was time to re-enlist, the soldier would often choose to do so, because we were not just focused on the soldier, but the family as well.

When I became garrison commander of one of the largest posts in the army, I was charged with overseeing the replacement detachment. This program was another version of a sponsorship program to integrate soldiers into the post and the community. What we found was, because the units were deploying so quickly, it was easier to centralize all the administrative tasks involved in transferring soldiers. That didn't relieve the individual units from providing sponsors though. We made sure that soldiers and families had sponsors to help them with unit and community integration from the very start and even set up a dedicated sponsorship cell for this purpose.

If you think this process sounds like a lot of work, you are correct. This energy is invested, though, for all the right reasons. We wanted the first touch point for a new soldier and their family to be a positive experience to help us to gain, build, and maintain their trust. The importance of this was easiest to see when I was garrison commander. That position gave me the perspective to compare the units with and without strong programs. The units with great sponsorship programs didn't have the personnel problems other units did; their soldiers had fewer legal, financial, and marital problems. As we "peeled back the onion," it was clear that sponsorship was the key and worked best when it started before a soldier and family even arrived at our post.

Does your organization have something like this in place? Do you go that extra mile to integrate a new employee into the organization and build trust with the new employee and their family?

When I came on as the Director of the Texas Veterans Land Board (VLB) for the State of Texas, we did not have a sponsorship program in place. I started with a training program to make sure all of us understood what our mission and vision was, who we were serving, and, more importantly, why we were serving them. After this training, we had the opportunity to welcome six new employees publicly.

A sponsorship program is hard to get started, but when your workforce understands the value of sponsorship, it is easy to maintain—especially when the employees you sponsored into the organization later become sponsors themselves. People want to feel special, and your employees *are* special, so invest the time and energy to build a great sponsorship program and start earning the trust of your new employees.

There's one more thing you should know about sponsorship programs: They become another tool in your marketing kit. As you train your new employee in the history of the company, its mission, and vision, you are building trust and, at the same time, marketing to them. They then, in turn, start marketing for you, no matter what position they hold in the company. I saw this with the VLB team. After we completed the training program and I felt comfortable everyone understood our mission and vision, we handed out VLB shirts for everyone to wear inside and outside the organization. What I have found is that every time I wear a shirt or a hat with the VLB logo on it, I inevitably get asked about it. If it is a veteran I am speaking to, they are a potential customer, and I can let them know about all the different benefits and services we provide. What is a better way to sell your product or service? Now, if everyone on my team is out there wearing a VLB shirt and they buy into our mission and vision, then I have just multiplied our customer reach exponentially. Because I have built a foundation of trust with the team, I have full faith and confidence that they will speak as highly of our organization as I would. They may not realize it, but everyone at VLB is on the marketing team.

TRUST IN THE EMPLOYEE

It is crucial that the employee trusts the organization, but the leaders of that organization must also trust the employees. They must trust every team member to do what is best for the organization if they want to be successful. This is our second pillar of trust.

There are two ways you, the leader, can gain trust in your workforce. The first is to give it to them upfront. On your first day, you go into the organization and announce that you trust they are going to try to do the right thing for the customer and the organization every time. You tell them you trust that they will provide you with all the information necessary to make sound decisions for the organization. The second option is to take away your employees' decision-making authority and make them earn your trust before giving it back. You tell your workforce that you will make all decisions until they have earned your trust, and then you will start to hand over the reins *or not*.

No matter which option you choose, you need to know that trust is a two-way street, but both directions are not equal. You can choose whether to give employees your trust or make them earn it, but you do not have that choice when it comes to compelling your employees to trust you. We will look at this more closely in the next section. For now though, remember that just because you have decided that you will trust your workforce from the start, it doesn't mean that you don't still have to earn their trust in return. They may not know you and being in a leadership position doesn't automatically give you a free pass here. So, whatever side of the fence you are on, know that you are still going to have to earn their trust and that's okay.

Now, each option can work. I have worked for leaders that have done it both ways, and I know which organization I would rather be a part of. I am going, to be honest with you I fall on the side of trusting first. Someone must be the adult in the room. Why shouldn't it be me, or you? The leader.

When I am in leadership positions, I choose to give my trust up front. As garrison commander, I started by gathering up my direct reports and letting them know they had 100 percent of my trust. I told them that I trusted they were going to help me train the workforce and make decisions that were focused on first class service. I made sure they knew I trusted them to come to me if there was a decision they believed I needed to make and that I trusted they would tell me the good news and the bad. I said that I trusted they knew and understood my philosophy and vision for the organization and would make decisions to execute them accordingly.

If you go this route, you must be ready to write off some mistakes. When I gave that speech to my direct reports, I fully understood this and knowing that our best teacher is our last mistake, I was okay with it. You should be too. You might end up having a not-so-pleasant discussion with your boss because your project lost some money. Or you may be forced to pick the best of some bad choices after a mistake. But wow, this can accelerate the creation of buy-in, and once you get that, you are off to the races. I am not advocating that you blindly give your trust; you can do this intelligently and reduce the risks by setting up monitoring processes (more on that in a moment). I am saying, though, that the not-so-pleasant discussion with your boss might be worth the buy-in you get from your employees when you prove you trust them.

I was able to reduce mistakes when I realized that, most of the time, they happened because I wasn't clear on my guidance, or when I didn't set up a good monitoring process to make sure a project wasn't going off the rails. They happened because of something *I* didn't do. I learned to engage in self-reflection before I blamed an employee and used the mistakes as a learning tool for both myself and the team.

There were times when I would have to come in and manage a project to get it back on track, but self-reflection taught me when to do this. Then, with a good monitoring process in place, I could get out of the way again and let the team work, knowing the same mistake would not happen again.

In the military, these types of monitoring processes are called CCIRs (Commander's Critical Information Requirements). A CCIR is a list of information that the commander tells the organization he will need to make a proper decision on any matter. CCIR is the criteria that you call and wake the boss, so he can decide what to do next. If you are in a high-performing organization, the staff has already planned options for the commander. An "if, then" concept. *If* this happens, *then* do this. Usually, it is an "*if, and, then*" scenario. *If* this happens, *and* this is in place, *then* do this. It doesn't always go smoothly, but that is what the staff works toward. The boss gets briefed on the CCIR and approves, so he knows what to expect if he does get a call in the middle of the night.

Let me give you a combat example of a CCIR. My unit had an operation in which we suspected insurgents were building improvised explosive devices (IEDs). We were concerned that if we tried to capture these insurgents, they would have backup coming in to support them, and there were several different ways that they could be coming, so we planned an approach with contingencies. We had our assault force (the unit that was going in to capture the insurgents), and we had a blocking force that would work on the most likely ways that enemy support could come from. We had a reserve force to either support the assault team or reinforce the blocking element. We put reconnaissance out to confirm or deny any supporting insurgent groups coming into the area along the most likely approaches, and then we had unmanned aerial vehicles (drones) watching the less likely avenues of approach. For additional help, we had planned indirect artillery targets and close air support.

After these elements were in place, I had only one decision to make: if, when, and where to use the reserve force. The CCIR was this: *If* the supporting insurgents came from a less likely approach *and* the assault force was executing their mission (in other words, they were successful and didn't need extra help), *then* I should move the reserve force to reinforce the blocking element to prevent penetration from the new insurgents. So, how did this CCIR help me trust my soldiers?

I knew I wanted to make the decision on when and where to put the reinforcing blocking force, but I didn't want to manage every aspect of the mission. I wanted to trust my units were going to do as directed. Having this CCIR in place let everyone know they had the freedom to execute their orders without my watching over their shoulder and gave me the reassurance that—even without watching every aspect—I would have the critical information needed to monitor the situation and make a good decision.

CCIRs are useful in other settings besides combat. In a business scenario, I trust that my direct reports can sign a contract for a needed service up to $500,000, but *if* it is $500,001 or more *and* we need to have the service, *then* I want to make the decision to sign it. Make sense?

In addition to CCIRs, you can use In Progress Reviews (IPRs) to monitor your business. These may not call for a decision, most likely not, but they give you a formal process to check in, make sure a project is on track, and have the information needed for any future decisions.

For example, you have a project that your organization is about to undertake. You brief everyone on the task at hand and explain why you are taking on the mission. The people who report directly to you give you initial feedback that your organization understands the task and the why, or you provide further details if there are any questions. Off they go to complete the project. Don't wait until the project is complete to find out how it went. Have an IPR to make sure your leaders are making the decisions you would make and that they're on track with the project. At each IPR, you can give a few course corrections or, if it is going particularly poorly, you can take over yourself, or hand it off to another organization.

The point here is that you receive updates as the project progresses. The deeper learning point is you can see if what you are saying is being heard. Your organization will listen to you talk all day long if you want (I hope you don't at this point), but are they *hearing* you? Do they understand what you want them to do? Do they understand why you want them to do it? Have they taken ownership of the project? IPRs let you see if and how each of your direct reports *hears* what you are saying, so you can adjust accordingly. Remember, as a leader, you are the head trainer, and although firing a low-performing employee is an option, how about training them first? Each of us *hears* or comprehends things in different ways. What I enjoy about being a leader is figuring that out and watching my direct reports find success. There is no better feeling. Well, there is, but this sure feels good!

TRUST IN THE LEADER

Trust in the leader from the employees is our final pillar of trust. How do you earn their trust? How do you earn their respect? Because that's what we are really talking about here. You respect them enough to give them projects and know they will complete them in a timely manner. They respect you enough to believe that you have their best interests at heart and will provide the resources and information they need to get the job done.

Let me give you a military example of a leader earning respect from his subordinates. At the time, I thought this was so simple and, quite frankly, what I thought any leader in my position should do. I was a light infantry company commander in charge of approximately 150 soldiers, and we were on a training exercise. Our mission was to defend our headquarters and prevent a group of tanks from crossing a bridge. This would give our higher headquarters time to rebuild and get back on the offensive.

Infantrymen hate defending anything because it's a lot of work to prepare a defense and you are static; you don't move from the defensive position. But that was our mission, so I picked our defensive positions, and we started to dig in. *Literally.* We dug in fighting positions (holes in the ground to about armpit level, so that you can fire your rifle) and built overhead cover, just high enough to see out, with a 36-inch layer of sandbags (to prevent artillery shrapnel from penetrating our defensive position). It was a lot of digging and filling sandbags. For all that work we used mainly modified shovels. A folding shovel that can be carried by the infantryman known as the E-tool (entrenching tool). We did get a backhoe for about four hours of the twenty-four it took to build our defensive position, and that helped, but not much.

I built my own position alongside my radio operators. They carried radios and lots of batteries—heavy batteries— wherever we went. It was a challenge for them, but I had to be able to talk to higher headquarters and to my units as well. Although there were three of us in the hole, only two could dig at any given time because one had to monitor the radios. We finally finished our fighting position. Now, was it to standard? That's debatable, but we decided it would have to do for the time being.

I went out to see how the rest of our defensive position was going. Usually, we build two-man fighting positions, so one person digs while the other provides security or lays concertina wire (razor wire). Concertina wire is used to funnel the enemy into our fighting positions or prevent them from coming into the protected perimeter around our headquarters. We laid what seemed like miles of concertina wire. We worked on constructing these defensive positions for almost 24 hours straight because we were taught to continue to improve your fighting position when able. When the sun came up the next morning, it was a sight to see. As I did the final checks on our perimeter, I knew there was no way the enemy was going to get into our position, let alone get across the bridge. In the unlikely event of a breach of our perimeter, the enemy would be funneled right into our fighting positions, which is exactly what we wanted the enemy to do.

The whole time we were building our defensive position, the enemy was trying to find us, so we got into a few skirmishes during that day and night. The reconnaissance I had put out the night before warned us that the enemy was coming, and come they did. It was a huge simulated battle that lasted for hours. In the end, we prevented the enemy from crossing that bridge and protected our headquarters.

As soon as the mission was over, guess who had to clean up the defensive position? Yep, you guessed it, we did. It was about noon, and this was our last mission of the field training exercise. The only thing preventing us from getting home was air and opportunity. That and the small matter of a defensive position that had taken almost 24 hours to build.

Now truth in lending, I had to attend an After-Action Review (AAR), a meeting to assess how the exercise went while my company was busy turning the defensive position back into a pristine wood line. I gave out a quick task and purpose. Task: Break down the defensive position. Purpose: So, we could go home. Simple, right? Off I went to the AAR.

An AAR is never a pretty sight. We intentionally beat ourselves up and discuss the myriad ways we could have done better. You are tired, it's standing room only in a tent or building that is usually unbearably hot, and the lights are always dim. All participants are fighting to stay awake to discuss what they did, how they did it, and what the outcome was. After what seemed like forever (actually about two hours), the AAR was complete, and we returned to our defensive fighting position. The company had done very well to that point and had most of the holes covered and sandbags and plywood stacked up. They were starting to work on removing the concertina wire.

If you recall, we laid out what seemed like miles and miles of concertina wire, and the wire is designed to get caught in uniforms, cause cuts, and generally make life miserable for anyone trying to get through it, or in this case, remove it. My leadership and I, along with the rest of the company, spent the next three hours taking down the concertina wire. We were all cut up, and our uniforms were ripped to shreds, but we finished the job relatively quickly.

Once we were cleared, we road-marched back to the company area, cleaned and stowed our weapons, accounted for and stowed the radios and other associated equipment, and had the final formation. I took the opportunity to talk to my soldiers and thanked them for their hard work. They had done a tremendous job throughout the field training exercise, and I was proud to be a part of such a great company. I handed control to my subordinate leadership to release the soldiers for the weekend, and off I went to my office to complete the paperwork that continues to happen even when you are away.

The following Monday, my first sergeant and I were having a cup of coffee before the first formation, and he told me that a bunch of soldiers had told him that they respected me for coming back to the defensive position after the AAR and helping with the breakdown. In the time, it had taken us to get back into the company area, my soldiers had talked to their colleagues in the other units. I don't know how they had the time or energy to talk after the intense field training, but they learned that some of the other leaders had not pitched in. I had earned their respect and hadn't done anything special my mind. I mean, I helped make the mess, so I had to help clean up the mess. That's the way my mom raised me. This simple act that gained the respect of probably the most scrutinizing part of my society at the time ... the infantrymen. All I did was live my philosophy, and I received so much in return. I had earned their trust and respect.

In that situation, the actions that led to earning my soldiers' respect came easy, and quite frankly, it should be easy.

Building trust in your organization and learning to trust your employees in return can be difficult, but this demonstration of commitment, if you do it authentically, can be simple.

You see, good leaders are authentic leaders. They are comfortable in their own skin and are aware of their strengths and weaknesses. Don't go out and fake it. Your people will see right through you. What I mean is that you cannot wake up one day and say, "I am going out to gain my workforce's trust," and then achieve it. It doesn't work that way. Instead, it is something you must strive for every day in a way that is native to you. Digging your own fighting position and pulling up concertina wire not your thing? That's okay. What is your thing? What do you feel comfortable doing to earn your employees' respect? How can you get into the trenches with them? Once you know, go out and do it. You will gain their trust and earn their respect and loyalty. Remember to keep doing it, because you need to maintain that trust. Trust is not a one and done, and it can be easily lost. But when you have the trust of your workforce, you are well on your way to buy-in.

TAKE ACTION

Make sure you understand what the three pillars of trust are and how you can foster them within your organization.

Pillar One: Trust in the organization

The employee must trust that the organization has their best interests in mind. Spend time developing your version of a sponsorship program for new employees and their families. Remember: You hire an employee; you retain a family. That's true even outside the Army. If you do not have a program in place yet, build one. Create a training plan to ensure that current employees know the history of your organization along with its mission, vision, and values. Then have a recognition ceremony for all who have completed the training and start multiplying your company's brand awareness. When people feel a part of the team, when they trust in the organization, they are happy to talk to just about anyone about it.

Pillar Two: Trust in the employee from the leadership

The leadership must trust the employee to do what is best for the organization. There are two ways to accomplish this: Give them your trust upfront or make them earn your trust. If you give them your trust and communicate who you are, this will develop quickly. Trusting the workforce to make decisions and solve problems on behalf of the organization will give you time to focus on the future of your company or focus your attention on areas that need your attention. And the risk of loss from mistakes is worth what you will gain in buy-in. Develop monitoring processes (CCIRs and IPRs) to ensure your workforce knows what decisions you want to keep at your level.

Pillar Three: Trust in the leadership from the employees

The employee must trust that the leadership is going to train and empower them to be fully engaged in the success of the company. You must earn your employees' trust every day.

While the other steps can be challenging, this should come more naturally because it is about earning respect by just being yourself. Remember, though, it is easy to lose this trust. Be authentic. Don't try to be someone you are not.

As you build trust in the organization, the employees, and the leaders, you will be able to share your vision for the business with them. That is what we will look at next.

5

STEP TWO: CLEAR VISION

Leadership is the capacity to translate vision into reality.
—LAO TZU

The task of the leader is to get his people from where they are to where they have not been.
—HENRY KISSINGER

During my service in the Army, I had the opportunity to observe and serve under leaders that had a clear vision of where they wanted their organization to go. I also saw other leaders really struggle with their vision. When that happens, an organization can still function, but wow is it difficult. A clear sense of purpose and knowing what you want

STEP TWO: CLEAR VISION

to achieve is incredibly powerful. You'll create an organization that can survive tough times as well as the good ones.

Why is articulating a clear vision so important? A clear vision is a great start in attaining commitment to the organization. It's tough to commit to something that is vague and fuzzy. In part, commitment comes from aligning your own values and beliefs with that of the organization. With a clear understanding of what you do and why you do it, you will find and retain those individuals whose own values align with your mission. You will build a workforce that is fully committed and believes in what you are doing and where you are going. That is what we want as leaders: engagement, which *Merriam-Webster* defines as emotional involvement or commitment. Can you see how this is connected to buy-in?

A clear vision provides a focus for the organization, a defined goal to attain within a specified time or, in military terms, an *end state*. A military end state that is articulated well conveys an understanding of what the leader wants the organization to look like, what the enemy looks like, and what the environment will look like once the time period or mission is complete. In a non-military scenario, the end state is not so different: It tells the employees what the organization looks like, what the competitors look like, and describes what the business environment looks like. A clear vision gives everyone in your organization their why and inspires them to make a commitment to themselves and their organization to ensure the company achieves that vision.

So, how is this end state communicated to the organization? In the Army, it is defined in a document called an Operations Order (OPORD). Nothing gets executed until the leadership writes, and the commander approves, the OPORD. The OPORD describes the situation, gives the mission, and details the supporting activities that need to be accomplished to meet the commander's end state. The OPORD has five paragraphs or sections:

1. *The situation* describes the friendly and enemy situation.

2. *The mission* details the task and purpose (or the what and why) of the mission.

3. *The execution* states the commander's vision and intent, including the tasks that need to be performed to complete the mission.

4. *Admin and logistics* list the support and equipment required to complete the mission.

5. *Command and control* define orders for how the mission will be commanded and the communications necessary to complete the mission.

All the paragraphs are important, but as a subordinate commander, I immediately went to paragraphs two and three to read the mission statement and the commander's intent. Within the commander's intent, I would usually find a more defined or expanded purpose, key tasks to be accomplished, and the end state that the commander wants at the end of the operation. Reading this would help me internalize the commander's vision and understand how my unit could support that vision.

Although the format you use to communicate your vision can vary from leader to leader, I recommend, at the very least, that you write down these two paragraphs: mission and leader's intent. Getting these thoughts down on paper will help your own clarity, which you'll then be able to transmit directly to your workforce. And these two items are essential to your subordinates' ability to carry out the mission.

I also recommend that you can gather input come from your subordinate leaders and staff. If they help write it, then they will completely understand it. It has also been my experience that if you can reach the workforce on an emotional level—which often happens when you involve them in this process—it will be a lot easier to get the company focused on attaining your vision and engaging them in making a better organization. You must decide what *your* vision for the organization is first, but seeking input once you are clear about what you want is beneficial to the mission and cultivating trust between yourself and your team.

When you write your vision, don't present your subordinate leaders with a manuscript full of run-on sentences and incomplete thoughts. This may make you feel that you have articulated your vision well, but your employees may feel confused. Even if you start with a longer draft, be sure to distill the mission and purpose down to their essence. A clear and brief statement will smooth the way for your workforce to internalize and implement the vision and fulfill your purpose, so make it concise enough to fit on a small card. And if you want your employees to sell your vision and the organization for you, make it easy for them.

After developing my vision for the VLB, we printed it on small cards and gave them to the workforce during our recognition ceremony when we also passed out shirts and welcomed the new personnel to the organization. The idea was that our staff could carry the vision card with them or post it in their work area. I wanted them to stay focused on what we are doing, why we are doing it, and how we are doing it, and where I want us to be at the end of our two-year vision (when we will revisit and evaluate where we are and where we want to go). Here is the vision we developed and printed on those cards:

The Texas Veterans Land Board Vision

VLB Mission (What and Why): The Texas Veterans Land Board serves Texas Veterans, military members, and their families by providing benefits directed by the people of Texas in appreciation and gratitude for service to the nation and our state.

VLB Philosophy (How): Honor each Veteran, military member, and their families with the care and respect they have earned through serving our nation, by developing and implementing meaningful programs, and ensuring that each Veteran, military member and family member is informed of all the benefits afforded to them by the State of Texas and the Federal Government.

VLB Vision (End State/Goal): Become the most trusted agency that Texas Veterans, military members, and their families turn to for support in not only our programs but all Veterans benefits programs.

We developed this vision through rounds of assessments and discussions with my subordinate leaders in the organization. Although our vision is stated in my words, it is a shared vision because of the process I used to derive and articulate it. Because I involved these leaders in developing our mission, I continued to build buy-in within the organization. At the end of the day, your leaders and workforce will execute the organizational vision as long as they buy-in to it.

ASSESSMENTS

The rounds of assessments and discussions we used to develop our vision at the VLB were a great tool. They helped me understand where we had been, so I could know where we were going. Listen to your workforce. Let them tell you what they do, how they do it, and why they do it. You may not agree with their current processes, but wait to make corrections when you understand *what* they are doing *why*. I understand time constraints, as you'll see in the final chapter, but do your best to hold off on corrections until you have the complete picture. Listen to understand first, then adjust later *if necessary*. Better yet, once you have finished your assessment, meet with your direct reports and inspire them to make the required changes.

Starting a new leadership position offers you a great opportunity to listen and make assessments. When I took the position of garrison commander, I had the luxury of talking with the outgoing commander to get his perspective on their current focus and where he would have shifted it, if they had more time and resources.

If you started your own company, or you have been in your position for some time, it's not quite the same, but you can always refresh your mission and vision. You may be so deeply involved in your company's logistics and processes that it's hard to see the forest for the trees. To gain a new perspective, consider asking from a peer, inside or outside your organization for a second opinion.

As a new leader or an old dog, you need to get out and let your team give you their assessment. I have found the best way to do this is with a standard question list. When I came into a new command position, I would ask my subordinates the following questions:

1. *What do you do and how do you do it?*

2. *Do you have everything you need to contribute to the organization?*

3. *What would you add if we had unlimited funding?*

4. *What would you do differently to make sure we are as efficient and effective as can be?*

5. *What do we do well and what can we improve?*

There are three main reasons for this line of questioning. First, I want to understand how the employees do what they do. But more importantly, I want to know if they understand why and how they fit into the company. Second, I want to know what we need to improve our organization. Finally, I want them engaged in the process of making the organization better from the beginning.

These questions are not exhaustive. You may develop additional questions to discover what you need to know to lead your organization to excellence. The main requirement is that the employees are engaging. At the end of the day, that is what we want: An engaged workforce that is part of a learning organization and is ready to adapt to change to achieve the organization's mission.

TAKE ACTION

1. Develop a clear vision.

Get your leadership involved in the process. Let them help you shape your vision. This will help you clarify your vision and ensure that the leaders within your organization understand it.

2. Help your workforce to internalize your vision.

Make the statement of your vision concise so it can be easily internalized by the workforce. If you can, limit it to one page; better yet, make it brief enough to fit on a small card. Post it throughout the area as a constant reminder to your workforce of what they are doing, why they are doing it, how they are going to do it, and what you want the organization to look like once it has attained the vision.

3. Modify your vision as needed.

Make your vision a living document, something that you review and modify as needed. If you have total success and reach your goal, then repeat the process and see just how far you can take the organization. At a minimum, review it every two years.

4. Get clear on where you need your organization to go.

Get out and assess where you are, so you know where you need to go. Get the workforce engaged and listen to what they have to say. Use the questions listed above.

———————

Once you have developed trust and a clear vision, you need to be able to communicate that to your team. That is what we will look at in the next chapter.

6

STEP THREE: COMMUNICATION

*The single biggest problem in communication is
the illusion that it has taken place.*

—GEORGE BERNARD SHAW

Trust and a clear vision are the foundations of buy-in, and your ability to communicate that trust and vision is the framework through which you cultivate buy-in. If you can't communicate what you want your organization to accomplish and that you trust your employees, then the company will fail to meet your expectations. If you want your team to share your vision, you need to show them what it looks like and that you believe they can carry it out.

One of the biggest challenges to effective communication is that one size does *not* fit all. As you probably already know, your workforce will consist of people with different strengths and abilities. They have been raised with different values, cultures, and levels of education, and more importantly, different ways of absorbing and processing information. This is not a bad thing. In fact, this is one of the things I appreciate about being a leader. I love figuring out how to work with the human dynamic in my organization and how best to relay information to them. The diversity of human nature makes it a challenge to find ways to inspire your workforce every day. What inspires one person may not inspire another, and you as a leader, must make the effort and stay curious about your people to be successful. Even more important than being successful yourself, is to make sure your workforce is successful.

Over the course of this chapter, we are going to consider this challenge and some of the things that may affect communication within your diverse workforce.

GENERATIONS

Within your workforce, you will probably find anywhere from two to four different generations. They all take in information and communicate in different ways. Traditionalists were born between the mid-1922 and 1945 and like to sit down and talk about other things before getting to the issue at hand. Baby Boomers were born between 1946 and 1964 and are more comfortable on the phone, or face to face than they are with email or other forms of communication. Members of Generation X, people born between 1965 and 1980 want to get to the point and move out. Generation Y or the Millennial Generation born in the 1981 and 1994 is comfortable with email, texting, Twitter, Facebook, Snapchat, or any other form of social media, as long as it is not face to face. These are all generalities, but the point here is, if you understand your workforce and their generational preferences, you will have a head start on knowing how best to communicate with them.

When I had the privilege to command the garrison at Fort Hood, Texas, I had all four of these generations in of my workforce. They spanned all departments (soldiers, the Department of the Army civilians, and contractors), and each department had its own communications standards. I also had the challenge of communicating with our customers. They all received and processed information differently and thus executed tasks differently.

Now, as you already know, I am not a "because I said so" type of leader, so I had to make sure I was communicating the "why I said so" effectively with all my staff. Because there was only one of me, and several thousand workforce members and several hundred thousand customers, I adapted my communication methods to suit them, instead of expecting them to adapt to me. This meant I spent a lot of energy trying to disseminate information. I used my direct reports for much of this, so I had a generational expert show them the best way to communicate with each generation inside their departments.

Because the workforce was so diverse and they all received information in different ways, we learned to use every form of media we had access to. If there was information I wanted to distribute to the workforce, I would call, email, post it on Facebook, submit it to our local newspaper, discuss it on our radio station, and have town halls. Your organization may not have its own newspaper or radio station, but I recommend you use every form of media you have available. Take this opportunity to find new ways to "get the word out." If you come across someone who says, "I didn't know," find out why and ask them what form of media they are most comfortable with. If it is a form of media you haven't used, then try it and see.

Town halls—large team meetings that everyone, regardless of department or rank, was encouraged to attend—are a form of communication that I started using when I had bad news to share, like budget or personnel cuts. The team needed to hear these things directly from me, and they needed to know how we address the issue and what we were going to do to help those affected by the negative news. I didn't want my team to think that every time we had a town hall it was going to be bad news, so I began holding them on a quarterly basis. Because of the size of my workforce and the hours they kept, I had to do several, but it was important enough to me to be able to talk with the workforce about the organization and continue to tell our story to the internal audience. Even if I did need to share bad news, I always highlighted what we were doing well, and mentioned team members who were being recognized throughout the Army and the Department of Defense for their initiatives, and discussed new initiatives that we were starting.

―――――――――

While town halls are great for communicating with large groups of people, sometimes email is not, and I want to give you a word of caution about mass emails to your whole workforce. Be very selective with the people that are authorized to write to your entire organization and the topics you want them to cover. Quite frankly, I would keep this authority at your level. If you send out mass emails several times a day, or even several times a week, on a myriad of topics, then it becomes spam and your team won't read it. Another danger is that the workforce starts to look to you instead of their manager for information. That contradicts everything this book is about. In my organization, we receive one mass email a week from our leadership. It is sent by the same person, and it is a simple one-page newsletter that highlights a few of the great things that have been accomplished during the week. It gives everyone situational awareness and helps to remind folks that there are a lot of people out there trying to make the organization better every day.

The last thing to remember when leading different generations is that, like trust, communication is a two-way street. The way your direct reports naturally communicate may not work for you, so it is your responsibility to teach them how you are comfortable communicating, so they can be understood. In my situation, I didn't want my direct reports to drop everything they were doing every time I reached out to them, so I let them know that if something was urgent, I would call. I told them that if there was information I needed that was not a priority, I would email and expect a reply within the week.

DEEDS, NOT WORDS

One thing is common to all generations of your workforce, including yourself— communication is about 80 percent physical and 20 percent verbal. The precise percentages depend on who you are talking to, but the point is that, while the receiver is listening to what you say, they also are *watching* how you say it. Human beings are visual in nature, so your body posture, the way you shake someone's hand, and your facial expressions when you are speaking with them are all visual cues that inform how people receive the information you are communicating.

Visual cues even extend to one of the most frequently used and misused forms of communication in today's age: email. How about that email that is in all CAPITAL LETTERS? It feels like you are being yelled at through your computer screen, even though you can't actually hear anything. I had a leader that wrote emails this way, and even if the email was only informational, my immediate response was, *"Why is this guy yelling at me?"*

Physical cues, in person and in writing, are important when delivering your message, but they are even more important when you aren't saying anything at all. What are you doing and what physical cues are you sending when you think no one is watching? I ask because, as a leader, you should understand that someone is always watching. So, are you practicing what you preach? Are you communicating through your physical deeds, not just your words?

A simple example in the Army is physical fitness. It is imperative that soldiers remain physically fit to withstand the rigors of living and fighting in combat. Every day, rain or shine, the first thing we do is Physical Training (PT). As a leader, if you talk about how important PT is in preparing for combat, you better be out there working out with your unit. You don't have to be the fastest or the strongest, but you better be out there because you are being watched. Let me give you an example.

When I was company commander at Fort Drum, New York, I learned about interesting weather phenomena like "lake effect snow" and "whiteout." Fort Drum is located near Watertown, New York, which sits next to Lake Ontario. Now, I must be upfront with you, I'm a warm weather guy. I would rather sweat all day than be cold.

Fort Drum has only about a month of summer a year. Okay … that may be an exaggeration, but it is cold most of the time. Not only is it bitter cold, but they get a lot of snow— lake effect snow to be exact. Lake-effect snow happens when a cold air mass moves across a large body of warm water. In this case, Lake Ontario, and Ft Drum sits right in the path of this type of snow. Did I mention they get a lot of snow?

For a bit of context, when I was stationed at Fort Hood in central Texas, even the possibility of snow, caused mass hysteria. (Did I mention I may be a little dramatic?) If we thought it might snow, we would shut the entire post down, and we certainly weren't going to do PT. We didn't have the equipment needed to clear the roads because the snow was so rare.

At Fort Drum, things were different. If it snowed, you dealt with it. There was a standing order that PT would be conducted outside unless the ambient temperature was 20 degrees below 0. Wind chill be damned, if it was *negative* 19 degrees, we were out in the weather doing PT. Sometimes we would get so much snow that the plows couldn't keep up, so we ran in the snow. I hated every minute of it, but I wasn't going to let my soldiers do anything I wouldn't do because that isn't how I was raised. And besides, I knew that, as their leader, the soldiers were watching me. So off we went, covered from head to toe in cold-weather clothes. At the end of the PT session, we would pat each other down to get rid of the ice that had formed on our clothes. Did I mention I really hate cold weather? It didn't matter. Often, it is through your deeds, not words, that you communicate with your team.

PERFORMANCE COUNSELING

A deed that will speak volumes to your workforce is the establishment of a performance counseling program. Later in this section, I will discuss what this type of program looks like, but for now, understand that it is a regular meeting (perhaps quarterly) where you ask open-ended questions of employees to take stock of where they're at and what they're working toward, as well as how you and the organization are performing. Its purpose is to continue to grow current or future leaders.

These meetings are an important part of the communication framework that supports buy-in for your organization. It helps you retain high-quality employees that are engaged in improving the organization. It is true that sometimes an employee and the organization just don't fit, but if, instead of firing an employee, you can retain and retrain them, it saves not only the financial cost of firing and hiring but also the emotional cost to other members of your team. When you fire and hire, rumors start about why the individual was fired, and folks start to get worried. If you have a good performance counseling program in place throughout your organization, you can alleviate a lot of anxiety.

You will notice I stated performance counseling, not evaluation. Evaluation is an important tool and should still be used, but if you have a good performance counseling program in place, then the evaluation is more of a formality.

I assume that you have already had initial training sessions—the type we discussed when we talked about trust and sponsorship—that lay out the vision, mission, and values of the organization. If you don't have that yet, implement that first. When that foundation is in place, you can move on to a performance counseling program that is practiced routinely and formally.

You make performance counseling routine, so the leader or future leader doesn't freak out when you suggest it. You make it formal by ensuring that it is a scheduled event on the calendar that the direct report is aware of. This allows the employee to prepare for the meeting. I recommend you do this quarterly, but you have to set that routine. Maybe it is monthly or semi-annually, but the sweet spot for me is quarterly. Once you have completed the first one, the employee will know what to expect during these meetings, and will come prepared to communicate and walk away with a plan for the next quarter.

In these meetings, I recommend that you break down the counseling into four parts, and allow about an hour to discuss all of them. The four parts are questions for your employee, and they are:

1. *What is going well (sustains)?*

2. *What needs work (improves)?*

3. *What are your goals for the next quarter?*

4. *What do I as your leader need to work on?*

Occasionally in the Army, I came across a performance counseling program that used these four components, or something similar but did so very poorly. They would have these long paragraphs that were already filled out, and the leader would tell the subordinate to read and sign it. That is not counseling. A better way to use these four components is to format them in bulleted topics, around three per component (but not necessarily), which you can use to facilitate a discussion. Then, you can simply write in highlights of the discussion. Quite frankly, the writing can get a little messy, but if counseling is done correctly, then there is input from both the leader *and* employee, and you want to capture that. With a pre-typed paragraph that the employee needs to read and sign, you miss the opportunity for the employee to *engage* in the counseling. As we know from discussing the concept of buy-in, *engagement* is what we want. An engaged employee knows how they are doing, wants to make improvements, and, by extension, makes the organization better.

The first two components will be answered through open conversation. In the third component related to goals,

I recommend you base your answers on *if, then* scenarios. And *if, then* scenario might say, *if* you attain this *then* you will receive this, or *if* you don't do this, *then* you will receive that. Examples are *if* you and your team grow sales by 10 percent, *then* you will receive a 10 percent bonus, or *if* you don't grow sales by 10 percent, *then* we may look at moving you into another area of the organization.

You will notice that in the fourth component, you receive feedback from your employee on how you are doing. This is a fact-finding mission. You need to know if you are being clear in your communications. Are you giving too much guidance? What can you provide for the employee to make them more effective and efficient? You can ask about any area you like, but your questions need to be engaging, not yes or no questions. Your employee might be a little surprised when you ask this question, but don't be afraid to ask, because you should want to know how to elevate and enhance the organization. Some of the observations you receive will be great, and others not so much, but in the end, you are engaging the employee as part of your own professional development.

End the performance counseling meeting by sending the employee away with a plan for the next quarter (or however long it is until your next scheduled meeting). That plan will be in the form of a copy of all your notes from the meeting, including details of their goals, and the consequences of accomplishing—or not accomplishing—those goals. It should be signed by you both. They get a copy, and you have a copy, and you will use that as you prepare for the next performance counseling session.

I scratch my head when I hear stories of employees or leaders who claim they didn't know they were going to be fired, or why they were fired. It is a travesty when that occurs. In an organization where there is effective communication and strong performance counseling, this could not happen. You can rest assured, that if you use these methods in your own organization, it will certainly never happen to you, and you will be well on your way to developing and benefiting from buy-in.

TAKE ACTION

1. Decide how you can best communicate information to your diverse workforce.

Examine your workforce from a generational perspective, and then hone in on how your employees prefer to receive information. Use every form of media you can. Train your leaders to do the same.

2. Let your direct reports know how you like to receive information.

You want your direct reports focused on leading their teams and not guessing how best to give you information. Make sure they understand what is urgent and what is not.

3. Set up a performance counseling program.

Make it a formal routine. Turn the meeting into a discussion and make sure there are clear expectations for the next quarter. There should be no surprises when an evaluation is completed or if you have to let someone go.

7

STEP FOUR: LEADERSHIP

A leader is one who knows the way goes
the way, and shows the way.
—JOHN C. MAXWELL

Leadership is the art of getting someone else to do
something you want done because he wants to do it.
—DWIGHT D. EISENHOWER

So, you already have or are working on, building trust throughout the organization. You have heard from your workforce, made an assessment, determined your vision, and communicated it clearly. Now it is time to sit back and watch the company grow and prosper, right? Not exactly. Now the real fun begins. You must lead through your deeds, not just your words. But what is leadership? We talked in the first part of this book about how leading is different from managing, but how do you *define* leadership?

In my future leader development classes, I asked attendees how they defined leadership. Everyone had different definitions that varied to a greater or lesser extent, and I didn't dispute any of them, because when it comes down to it, your definition of leadership and your leadership style is your own, and you have to be comfortable with it. Some of the definitions people offered were very long because they wanted to capture everything that defines leadership. That was all good, and it allowed everyone in the class to understand how others defined leadership.

In the end, though, I think defining leadership is very easy if you strip it to its core. My definition of leadership is "getting people to do stuff." It's very simple, I know, but I think that is what leadership is. You can inspire people, you can motivate them, you can make people do what you need them to do, but in the end, it is all about "getting people to do stuff." The definition is simple, but the execution is difficult. That's what we're going to look at in this chapter.

LEADERSHIP PHILOSOPHY

Everything you have read so far in this book has laid the groundwork for you to be a great leader. Now, if you want to get people to do stuff, you need to develop a leadership philosophy and get it out to your subordinates. A leadership philosophy gives insight to the leader. It is separate and distinct from a vision. A leadership philosophy is what makes the leader tick, what the leader believes, what their values are, and what is important to them. This philosophy will inform every action you take as a leader, and understanding it up front will make all your decisions easier. This doesn't have to be a long document or a book. In fact, you should keep it as simple as you can, for the same reason your vision should be clear and concise—you want your subordinate leaders to be able to grab hold of it, share it, and eventually start modeling it in their own approach to the organization.

I believe that we all have a philosophy on how we approach the challenges and opportunities of life and leadership. We have a baseline set of values and beliefs that we turn to in good times and bad times. Whether you know it or not, you already have a philosophy that, consciously or subconsciously, you exude physically, mentally, and spiritually. It is what is important to you. You want to become conscious of this philosophy so you can communicate it to your leaders and the organization at large, so they know what those values and beliefs are and can hopefully align their philosophy, at least at work, with yours.

In the Army, leaders are taught to become conscious of their own philosophy by writing it down and sharing it with the organization, to inform the unit how the commander thinks, and what they feel is important. Army leader philosophies almost always align with those of the wider organization since we all come from the same training background and Army values are ingrained in us from the beginning of our career.

As I came into garrison command, my initial thought was that I had to write some grand document that covered a wide range of topics, since garrisons have such a broad mission. As commander, I oversaw everything from public works, to human resources, and training enablers that help our soldiers get the most out of training. There was the quality of life support in the Morale, Welfare and Recreation Division, the budget management of millions of dollars to run an army post, caring for soldiers that have an addiction or behavioral health issues, police, fire, and rescue and much more. I just knew I was going to have to write a book to pass on my philosophy to my diverse workforce. However, when I looked at my higher commander's philosophy, I had the "aha" moment on how to convey my philosophy accurately to my command by keeping it very simple. I still carry the 3x5 card with my former commander's philosophy in my pocket to this day, and I do my best to mirror that philosophy every day as the Director of the VLB. I wish I was savvy enough to have thought of this on my own, but my boss had already done it, so why re-invent the wheel? I decided that if the commander of all the installations in the Army located around the world can keep it simple, then so could I.

Here is my philosophy:

1. *Build your teams through trust and empowerment of subordinate leaders.*

2. *Do your best. Do what is right.*

3. *Take care of your people and they will take care of you. Say thank you often.*

4. *Know the standard, enforce the standard, and train your people.*

5. *Demonstrate inspired leadership every day. Get out there, be seen, be heard, and listen.*

6. *Never quit.*

Simple, right? But very powerful as well. I believe this philosophy can be used at any level of leadership, in any organization, and will make the leader and the organization successful when applied. These six points should tell your subordinate leaders, right from the start, how you are going to conduct business and what you expect from them as they conduct their business. If you—and they—live by this philosophy, you will create the environment needed for buy-in throughout your organization.

Let's look at each of these six points, in turn, to see exactly how they create buy-in.

1. Build you teams through trust and empowerment of subordinate leaders.

We already discussed how to build trust within the organization, between you and your employees. We also examined how to empower your future leaders, while learning to let go and trust while monitoring. To truly empower your subordinate leaders, you need to train them to be *good* leaders. Don't just deliver the ol' "try hard and do good" speech. Set them up for success by training them and giving them the tools they need to become a good leader for your organization.

As garrison commander at Fort Hood, setting up my subordinate leaders and future leaders for success was difficult sometimes. One area under my command was the Department of the Army Civilians, and I focused on building our future leaders on that side of the house first.

The soldiers constantly had opportunities to develop professionally, and I felt that the Army civilians—who support the soldiers—should have the same opportunities. They did, have a program already, but it was not very successful. They had brought in some superb leadership trainers, but the cost was significant. It was money well spent in my opinion, but it was money we couldn't afford. Because of the cost, they could only do it once a year, and our higher headquarters were asking questions about the return on investment. Although I believed the existing program was money well spent, we needed a program we could use more often, to train more future leaders to step into positions of higher responsibility when called upon.

I came up with some ideas and immediately got pushback. My superiors said it would cost too much, and the organization couldn't afford to have people away from their positions for that long. We all agreed that we needed a better training program, but it had to be affordable in time and money. Using this criteria we developed a new program that offered three courses annually and cost significantly less than the old program. I couldn't do anything about the workforce's time away from their positions, but I didn't mind, because I considered the training an investment. The training programs create buy-in from your existing workforce and the time and money is well worth it compared to the cost of hiring and training a new employee.

The three annual courses were not enough, though, for the well-rounded approach that I thought this program needed. I wanted our future leaders to be trained not only in good leadership, but also learn what their counterparts were doing in other parts of the garrison; it's important for everyone to understand where they fit within the organization overall and to understand how others fit too.

My leaders and I decided on a course that would be three months long, with attendees attending one or two classes per week. To ease the costs, all the classes were taught by leaders within our organization; we wouldn't have to pay anyone to teach. This gave me the opportunity to involve our leaders and gain their buy-in for the program, while allowing our future leaders the opportunity to see, hear, and learn from current leaders across the organization. As the program got underway, I was amazed at the positive comments about this part of the training.

The classes were the perfect opportunity for me to talk to our up-and-coming leaders in a small class, so they could hear, in a different mode of presentation, my philosophy and how I approach leadership. They could ask questions, and I could hear and answer their concerns. With about 25 attendees in each class, everyone had the opportunity to learn about each organization within the garrison and take a tour to see what each directorate and their organizations did in support of our soldiers and their families. They were taught the processes and procedures that we used to accomplish missions, and the Army's military decision-making process, which we utilized to prepare for missions that we had coming up. The directorates also had the opportunity to discuss their own leadership philosophy with each class. Afterwards, we had the attendees develop their own personal leadership philosophies.

One intangible benefit was that people in the classes established relationships with one another. They could put a face with a name when they had to call and work through an issue together. We celebrated class completion with graduation ceremonies, and the former graduates attended the ceremonies to expand and improve even more relationships. These were our future leaders, so we made it a big deal. We invested our own time and energy in the classes, and we wanted to ensure that our graduates knew that we had new expectations for them. We expected them to use their new training to be problem solvers and deep thinkers while they supported the garrison mission.

The takeaway here is, in order to empower your people, you must train them, and if there is a will, there is a way. It was difficult for me to work against my superiors' pushback, but I knew we needed a future leader's development course, we just needed to figure out how to do it in a cost-effective manner. The program we developed *was* cost effective, only ten percent of the previous program's cost. The other benefit of doing a leadership course in-house was that the directors had the opportunity to get in front of our future leaders who, in turn, got to know our leadership throughout the garrison. In the end, I think we made the leadership course much better than what we had before.

2. Do your best. Do what's right.

The second point of the leadership philosophy I adopted does not require new programs or formalities. It is about *attitude.* I have never expected perfection from myself or my leaders, but I have always tried my very best and expected the same from them. If you have communicated a clear vision, given your team their why, their purpose, and where you want them to take the organization, and you are creating and cultivating buy-in throughout your organization, then you can trust your team will do what's right.

Once you are confident that you and your team are doing their very best, it becomes easier to investigate issues with customer service, productivity and so on. When you know the problem *isn't* that they aren't doing their best, you know to look inward. I would ask, *Do my people understand the purpose of their piece of our organization? Do they know me and my philosophy and understand our organization's mission?* Nine times out of ten, I realized the problem happened because I hadn't been clear. This would become a learning opportunity for me and the employee.

A perfect example of this comes from my current position. When I joined the VLB, I made a lot of organizational changes, and I put some people in new positions, ones that I thought played to their strengths, and I tried to give the clearest guidance I could. In one case, I missed the mark. I knew this person did her best and wanted to do a good job, but I realized I hadn't done a good enough job of clearly defining what I wanted her to do. She was frustrated, I was frustrated and it wasn't an ideal situation. We had the opportunity to talk at our performance counseling meeting, and we clarified what I wanted her to do and why. Since gaining a common understanding, we have both been very happy with the work she does for the organization.

3. Take care of your people and they will take care of you. Say thank you often.

I can give you two main reasons why taking care of your staff and thanking them is important. First, they deserve it. They are the primary reason for the success of your organization and quite frankly, they are the reason you exist. If you think about it, you cannot say thank you too often. Second, as the statement says, if they feel cared for, they will care for you and the organization.

Providing for your team doesn't mean you must coddle them, but you should try to create an environment that will allow them to have even greater success. Make sure they are paid their due. Ask yourself, *do they have everything they need to be successful in the position they are in?* And that doesn't just mean equipment and tools, but education and training too.

When I was a lieutenant in the Army, I had a company commander who taught me a valuable lesson in taking care of our team. I was second in command of the company, which had a little over 200 personnel. One of them was a sergeant who needed to attend a course to help him get promoted to the next rank. If he were promoted, we would lose him to another unit that needed his skill set and rank. We were preparing to deploy to the National Training Center (NTC) in California, and the sergeant, who was extremely talented, would miss the NTC training to go on his course. NTC is in the middle of the Mojave Desert, a miserable place to train, because of the harsh elements and the well-trained opposition forces (OPFOR) your unit is pitted against. They have a team of controllers who observe just about everything your unit does or doesn't do, and even if your unit does well, they will find your weak spots. When your unit deploys to NTC, it is kind of like heading to the Super Bowl.

I was concerned that our skilled sergeant would not be there to support the unit, but my commander had words with me. He reminded me that if this sergeant passed his training and got promoted, he would become a very positive asset for his next unit. It would be a good thing for him and his family, and it would be good for the army as a whole. My commander also asked me to consider the trust we would gain from not only the sergeant, but also the rest of our unit. They would know we had put the needs of the soldiers before that of the unit. That is a big time win for everyone. My commander was right, and in the end, we did just fine at NTC. The sergeant progressed through the ranks and eventually became a command sergeant's major, the senior enlisted person in a brigade of over 5,000 soldiers. The point here is to focus on the health and welfare of your people so they can stay focused on making your organization great.

4. Know the standard, enforce the standard, and train your people.

Like me, my boss—the one who wrote this philosophy— led thousands of people. For either of us to know the details of how every process in our organization worked, or how every procedure was conducted was a tall order and, quite frankly, not necessary. You do not have to be the resident expert of all the components of your organization, but you *should* have a good understanding of the standards involved with all those processes. If, like most leaders, you have not previously worked in every department or division, understanding these standards will take some time. As garrison commander at Fort Hood, I was still learning after three years on the job. In fact, the learning never ends, but that is not a bad thing. Let me ask you, what better way is there to interact with your workforce than to let them show you how they do what they do? Getting out there will let you communicate and earn more trust from your workforce while learning what the standards are so you can then enforce them.

When I reported to my first unit in the Army, I was introduced to the expected standards through a two-week training cycle that culminated in a test to earn the Expert Infantryman's Badge (EIB). This test is not easy, and for infantrymen, other than combat badges, there is no greater honor than to earn the EIB. At that point in my career, this was a *huge* event, and at first I looked forward to it. That is, until I met my new company commander. He welcomed me to the unit with one caveat I would only take over as a platoon leader if I earned the EIB. I was concerned

The test takes one week, and the evaluators assess you on all the skills an infantryman must know to be successful in training and on the battlefield. During the testing, you have to follow each step of each task in order, or you fail that task. If you fail more than two tasks, you are out of the running to earn the EIB. I recall that there were 35 tasks we had to complete, which ended with a 12-mile ruck-march and an assessment on clearing, disassembling, assembling, and performing a function check on an M16 rifle.

The pass rates for the EIB back then were in the teens and twentieth percentiles, so the testing was stressful for all of us, and it was made worse by the constant rain. (Of course, every time an infantryman goes out to train, it rains.) What I didn't realize at the time was that the company commander's requirement was a blessing in disguise. I was able to build trust with my platoon and show them what I stood for, my expectations, and my vision right away. I was the new guy, I had missed all the train-up, but I was out with my men, and we trained and tested together. I can think of no better way to get to know your right-hand man than to share shelter halves (think one-man tent once you get the two halves together) and live with him for two weeks. We were bonding as a team, and it was incredibly important, because just six months later, we were getting ready to deploy to Operations Desert Shield and Desert Storm.

Now, I was lucky. I had an excellent company commander. He knew just when to appear and see how the platoon and I were doing. He would talk with us while we were waiting to go to another station or on break. He was always upbeat and you could never get him down. Detailed to a fault, he was the first leader who taught me that it was okay to fail, so long as you learned from it and didn't do it again. He taught me that you never know how far you can go with anything if you don't go to failure, so why not do your best, see how the chips fall, learn from it, and get better? All this was true, but still, he told me that if I didn't get my EIB, I didn't get my platoon.

By the second week of training, I was doing well and had passed all the different tasks. Then I came to the hand grenade station. The first part of the test was to identify all the grenades in the Army inventory-check. The second part required that we maneuver to an enemy bunker and properly throw the grenade into the bunker. I should say, these were training grenades. They felt like the real thing, but had a small fuse so we could continue to use the body of the grenade again and again. The third and final part of the grenade station had caused a lot of infantrymen to fail out of the testing. You had to get to a covered position and throw a hand grenade thirty-five meters into a hole with a five-meter circumference. You had three grenades for this testing, and at least one of them needed to explode within the hole. Although grenades are around and about the size of a baseball, they have a stem that causes them to go in all different directions when thrown, so you never knew if they were going to make it into the circle.

With my first grenade, I low-crawled on my belly to the protected fighting position, looked up to see where the circle was, and dropped back down. I pulled the pin on the grenade, got up on my knees, shouted "grenade," and threw it toward the circle. I dropped back behind the position and heard the grenade go off. I was immediately told to try again because it had gone in the circle and bounced right out. I had two grenades left and was getting nervous. Thoughts raced through my head of being put out of the testing for *this* ... for failing to throw a grenade into a circle!

On my second try, I went through all the steps mentioned before and threw the grenade. I heard the boom immediately followed by someone telling me it had gone long. *Crap!* I had let my nerves get to me and thrown it long! I couldn't believe it. *What would my men think? What would my company commander do?* Would he really not let me have the platoon? I had one last shot.

Although it was February, it was February in Texas, and I am sure the temperature was in the 40s or 50s. From my perspective, though, sitting behind that position with only one grenade left, and my platoon on the line, it felt as if it were 100 degrees with 99 percent humidity.

My mind continued to race as I began to maneuver to the protected fighting position again. I went through the steps, took a good long look at where I needed to throw the grenade, popped down, pulled the pin, got back up, hollered "grenade," and threw it approximately three feet in front of my position—far from the circle. I watched as it hit the ground, then dropped down behind my protected fighting position. I knew I was done. I just knew it. My career was over before it had started. I felt like Goose from *Top Gun* when he asked Maverick for the number to the trucking company for his new career. I heard the boom of the grenade exploding and looked up. Somehow, some way, it had rolled all the way into the circle before going off.

Everyone, even the instructors, were amazed that it had made it into the circle. Soldiers told me, "You are one lucky lieutenant, sir." I wasn't going to argue. I wanted to get off that station as quickly as I could. I was elated, but as I mentioned before, this station took out a lot of infantrymen, including a lot of soldiers from the platoon I hadn't yet earned, so I had to stay calm and console some of the men who hadn't passed that station.

By the start of the last day, most units, including our platoon, had thinned out, and only a few of us remained for the 12-mile ruck-march. For this exercise, you carried 35 pounds in your rucksack, and you needed to complete the 12-mile march within three hours. When I think about that weight now, it seems like nothing compared to what our soldiers carry in combat today. All that equipment is crucial because it protects the soldier, but it is heavy.

Still, at the time, it was a considerable weight to carry. Once our rucks were loaded, we headed down a six-mile path, turned around, and came back. My company commander was there to ruck with us, taking each step and motivating those who began to fall behind. I am sure he could have completed it easily on his own within two hours if he had wanted to, but he was there to motivate and make sure those of us that had made it this far, finished. We did and we were successful at the M16 station that followed. As soon as the last person completed the testing, we immediately had an awards ceremony.

Out of a battalion of more than 600 men, approximately 40 of us earned the EIB that day. Through this experience, I earned the trust of my men. They got to know me in extreme conditions, and I got to know them. Although only a few received the EIB, all of us were better for the training. And I got to keep my platoon!

It was this intense training and testing that quickly taught me the standards expected of an infantryman. Earning the EIB gave me the confidence to enforce those standards throughout my career. Although I wasn't always personally training my men, I knew that—because I enforced the standards— they were being trained in the fundamentals of being an infantryman.

5. Never quit.

This is a key point in my leadership philosophy because you encounter so many obstacles that might tempt you to give up. Unexpected challenges, hemorrhaging funds, and a lack of employee buy-in. These are only a few of the things that could make you want to quit caring, quit investing your energy, quit improving, or even quit the job. But one of the worst things that make leaders want to quit is the naysayers.

Unfortunately, you'll encounter a lot of naysayers in the world: in the civilian or military world, and your personal and professional realms. If you try to break from the norm, they protest and say, "No, we're not doing it that way. We'll do it the way it's always been done." I've always hated that statement. Whenever I've heard it or something like it, I'd think that the organization had lost its purpose. So, I would ask, "But *why* do we do it this way?"

One of my biggest naysayers was my attorney. Garrison commanders, who oversee several thousand staff members and have considerable authority, were encouraged to work with attorneys to protect themselves, their staff and the Army as a whole. This is affectionately termed CYA (Call Your Attorney). When I was in that role, I rarely acted without calling my attorney, and he would always be the devil's advocate. This was as it should have been. His job was to be prudent and cautious, and he was very good at his job.

Initially, when I would get a hair brained idea running through my head, I would ask my attorney, can I do this? Nine times out of ten he would say, *NO*. After a few rounds of this, I figured out how to get the answer I needed to move forward. I needed to ask, *How can I do this?* Once I reframed my question, it was as if the heavens opened, and my attorney would provide me with a step-by-step action plan on how I could do something that was somewhat unconventional. Later, I asked him why he hadn't just told me how I could accomplish what I wanted to do from the very beginning. His reply was pure gold. He said, "That is not the question you asked me. You asked *could I* rather than *how can I*. As any good attorney, would do, I answered the question and only the question."

This is something to think about if you work frequently with an attorney in your business. I recommend that you do consult with an attorney on almost everything you do. They can be great sounding boards for you as you work through challenges.

This conversation with my attorney taught me about the ultimate question: *How can we do it better?* It is the question that will help you win over the naysayers. When you are out there leading and you see something that doesn't seem right, smell right or feel right, start asking questions, and end with the ultimate question. How can we do it better? Once you earn the reputation that you will find a way, the cynics will disappear, your workforce will open up to you and they will provide you with sound advice on how to improve operations. At a minimum, allowing your workforce to speak freely will let you know what they are thinking, and then you can explain why you think something should be done in a particular way. They learn a lot about you, and you will learn a lot about them and the subject at hand. It's a win-win, right? Never quit—not in the face of naysayers, defeatists, complainers or anyone else.

6. Demonstrate inspired leadership every day. Get out there, be seen, be heard, and listen.

To create buy-in, I believe you should inspire your people. Inspiration is the best way to get people to engage with you, your philosophy and your vision. To inspire others, you must be inspired yourself, so you need to find your own inspiration every day.

One of the easiest daily routes to an inspiration that I found came when I was living on post as garrison commander at Fort Hood. Almost every day, my German shepherd and I would get up and run early in the morning, real early… some would say crazy early (at least, my wife did). We would be out beating the pavement before the soldiers started to arrive on post, and I found the quiet and calm soothing as we ran our route. Except for an occasional train going by, and my heavy breathing as I plodded along, it was a sleepy post that began to come alive as our soldiers started to show up for daily Physical Training. My dog and I would finish our run just as reveille sounded across the post. As we cooled down, we would hear cadence being called as the soldiers headed out for their morning run. It would start as a low murmur off in the distance, and as more units began their runs, the cadence would turn into a loud roar.

It reminded me of the power of the soldier and how it grows as we come together. One soldier is incredibly powerful, but as they come together, 30, 100, 1,000, 10,000 and more soldiers singing cadence in unison, that roaring sound made me feel confident that our army, and our nation, was going to be just fine no matter what comes our way. In those moments, more than any other, I knew that the American soldier would stand ready to defend against those that may want to do us harm. We were preparing every day for that call. It was *inspiring*.

I will admit, it was easy for me to be inspired every day because I was a soldier and I loved what I did and what I was a part of. Being a soldier was not the only thing that gave me energy and motivation though. I was also inspired when I visited our Child Development Centers, watching our caregivers provide a quality of care unmatched by any center in the civilian sector. They truly cared for the children, and they loved to contribute in this way. A lot of the caregivers were spouses of soldiers, and they provided the same level of care that they expected when they dropped off their child off at 5:00 in the morning because mom and dad need to be with their units for PT. They understood the hardships of raising a family in the military, and they took care of those children as if they were their own. They didn't do it for recognition; when I did recognize their hard work and commitment, they were so surprised that it was usually a big "boo hoo" fest. (Did I mention I even cry at Walmart openings?)

These things inspired me to provide the best leadership I could for my organization. They helped me to be "switched on" every day. Inspirational moments like these are everywhere. Sometimes you have to go look for them, but I would bet that you can find them throughout your experience on a daily basis. Seek them out and inspire yourself so you can inspire others. That's how you achieve buy-in. You have to inspire yourself before you can expect to inspire others. So, what's your inspiration?

GET OUT AND LEAD

No matter how inspired you are, you will not inspire anyone else if you hide in your office. You must get out and lead. You need to be heard and seen if you want to motivate your workforce and lead your organization to success. Sounds obvious, right? There are many leaders who don't do this. They spend their time managing, not leading (as we discussed at the beginning of this book), or they sit in their offices thinking of good ideas that most likely will come to nothing. To lead effectively you cannot hide. You must get out and sell your vision to your workforce every single day.

As a leader, you are selling the organization to your customer, but you must also sell yourself to the organization and even sell the organization to the workforce. To do this, you must be the best salesperson in your organization. Everyone you sell to, inside and outside the organization, will be watching you. It is a fact of life, so you need to be switched on every day. You may think to be constantly on sounds exhausting, but it does not have to be. Being inspired helps. Being authentic helps too.

In fact, when you are being authentic, being on really isn't that hard. I know from experience. That's why you must be yourself. Don't try to be someone else. Know your strengths and weaknesses. How do you know what they are? You should be brutally honest with yourself. Then verify with friends or, better yet, those you may not necessarily get along with. In the Army, we used a 360-degree review from superiors, peers, and subordinates to help us see ourselves more clearly. These reviews weren't perfect, but they were another avenue to find out our strengths and weaknesses. Once you are aware of your own, you can enhance your strengths and work on your weaknesses.

Knowing my strengths and weaknesses, and feeling comfortable in my own skin was what kept me afloat when I was first promoted to garrison commander of one of the largest installations in the Army. It was a sink or swim situation, and I didn't have much else to cling to.

You see, there is no military school that teaches you how to be a garrison commander. I had been trained to be an infantryman, and that was exactly what I was for most of my career. The army does have a school for most promotions. With my very first promotion to platoon leader, I went to an Infantry Officers Basic Course to learn the ropes. I later attended the Infantry Captains Career Course to learn how to be a company commander. Over the course of several years, I was sent to the Command and General Staff College to learn how to be an operations officer, an executive officer, and eventually an infantry battalion commander.

When I found out I had been selected to be a garrison commander, I started to ask questions about which school, or course I could attend so I could learn how to be a garrison commander. There wasn't one. Not one that I could attend, anyway. The Installation Management Command, which was my higher headquarters, did have a Garrison Commanders Course, but they didn't want me to attend until I had been in the garrison commander's seat for at least a month to provide some context to understand what the course would teach me. Instead, they sent me to the Brigade Commanders Course. That was two weeks of learning how to be an infantry brigade commander, which was great, but not much help in preparing for garrison command.

I felt like a fish out of water when I started my new role. I was lucky though. My team was comprised of incredibly talented civilians, and a lot of them had previously served in the Army. They could at least translate "garrison speak" for me, which is a whole different language than what I'd grown up around. They had acronyms for acronyms, and when I took command, it was all Greek to me.

I had no experience being a garrison commander, but I did know how to lead, and I knew that sink or swim, I was going to be authentically me. I was going to use my strengths to keep me afloat.

I decided to get out and lead and be the best salesman in my organization. I left my deputy to manage the garrison, so I could get out and sell my vision to the workforce. I wanted them to think like I did and react to situations as I would, and the only way I could do that was to be among them and lead. I didn't give orders. I listened and asked open-ended questions, to encourage them to tell me what they thought. I didn't know the garrison, but I did know its customers (which included infantrymen), so I spoke from the customer's perspective. I let my leadership know what I wanted our organization to provide: first class customer service. The only way to let my leaders and workforce know this was to talk with them. Every chance I got, I demonstrated my commitment to customer service by letting them show me how to provide the type and level of customer service that was our mission.

By listening to them and communicating my vision regularly, we had a base from which to communicate. They may not have agreed with every part of the vision, but they knew I wanted to provide first class customer service to all the soldiers and families of this installation. We didn't achieve this standard overnight. It took weeks and months of going out to see the 15 different directorates within my organization. I had to learn the standards of each directorate, and how and why they did business the way they did. Then I had to sell my vision back to them. Truth be told, it took time, but it wasn't that hard. We all wanted the same thing. We were motivated by the knowledge that we were taking care of our nation's treasures and their families. What I hoped they would take away from our discussions was that I trusted them. I wanted them to know I was comfortable with their decision making, and I was fully aware that they wouldn't always be right, but that was okay because we would learn from our mistakes.

What began to happen was, I had a workforce that wasn't afraid to think on their feet. They made things happen on their own. They solved issues before they became problems. Because of the size of the installation and breadth of our mission, I required a workforce that could respond quickly. I knew that if they waited for me to decide, then the momentum we needed to maintain would come to a screeching halt. I didn't want that. I wanted to empower our customer service providers with the authority to figure it out—whatever "it" was—and get it done. As the months went by, while I was getting out there and communicating, this started to happen.

I began to see a much more positive trend in our customer service surveys. Just as important, I started to see more positive feedback from the workforce. I observed a shift in ownership, from waiting for the boss to decide to a can-do attitude that said, "I've got this, and here's what we are going to do." If they were providing the customer with the best service they could, they were meeting my vision for the organization. Because I had been out there sharing my vision, they knew that this was the attitude I was looking for.

It wasn't all rainbows and lollipops. I had my own naysayers within the organization and some directorates took a little longer to buy into my vision than others, and that was okay. Whenever they questioned my vision, it gave me the opportunity to reiterate why I wanted to do business this way. Eventually, they all bought into my ideas.

A perfect example was with my resource manager. She was an amazing woman who was extremely competent. As she started to buy into the vision I was selling, something wonderful began to happen. I saw this shift in a unique way. Every year, the garrison had to plan the next year's budget, and she would reach out to the directors to get their best guess of how much they needed and she would plan accordingly. There were never enough funds, but she would break it out and work with the directors to make sure everyone had what they needed if not everything they wanted. By the time I saw the budget, she had already made most of the decisions. The directors had input into the budget and they may not have been thrilled with the results, but they could see that it was done in a fair and equitable way and per my priorities. The decisions were made before I saw the final product. The truth is, I am a lot smarter when someone has the answer for me already.

It wouldn't have been that way if my resource manager didn't buy into my vision. She could have come to me first and let me figure out who needed what, and the process could have dragged on forever. It wasn't like that though. She understood my vision and knew my priorities (as did all the directors), and she worked it out on her own. I would receive an information brief rather than a decision brief. She would call it a decision brief, but the decisions were already made. The two questions I asked were, "Did the directors provide input, and did they agree with the budget?" The answer was always that they weren't happy, but they had given their input, and all concurred with the final budget. Then I would ask one more question: "Where do I sign to approve the budget?"

That's what buy-in can get you as a leader. You get a lot of information briefs rather than decision briefs, and I believe this is a good thing. It confirms that your workforce is engaged and that they have taken ownership of their mission, and they feel empowered to make decisions without waiting for the boss. It can be a lot of work to get to this point. It requires that you focus your time and mental energy on the workforce, but the dividends you receive as the leader are well worth the effort.

Depending on the size and scope of your organization, and the momentum of operations, it could be quite some time before you get an opportunity to walk among your employees, to lead and sell your vision. During that time, some bad decisions may occur, or at least decisions you wouldn't have made. You must be prepared for that. You must be willing to write it off as I mentioned in the chapter on trust. If you can use it as a learning experience for you and your workforce, writing it off should not be a big deal. Then you can get back out there, leading, and selling. You can take the chance to spend time with your workforce, selling your vision.

If bad decisions continue to be made then, as I said before, look inward first. How could you have sold your message better? Use everything that comes up as a learning experience, and go out and meet with your workforce again, and *learn with them*. Your communication skills will improve, and so will their understanding of your vision.

If an individual repeatedly makes mistakes, then it may be time to help that individual find other employment. It is not lost on me that in the corporate world, the bottom line is crucial, and mistakes cost money. But if you can, deal with missteps before they affect the bottom line and turn them into valuable learning experiences that will save time and money in the future. You will show trust in the employee and obtain buy-in not only from that employee but also from those around them.

Learning experiences are not restricted to just the workforce. I found that taking this approach with our customers was also enlightening and it drove a lot of my interactions with them, which gave me useful information to bring back to my workforce. I knew that if we wanted to provide first class customer service, then we all needed to shut up and listen to those customers we were serving. I used each customer interaction, whether positive or negative, as an opportunity to gain valuable feedback. I asked the customers, *why* fairly often to start a dialog with them. Initially, in those conversations, I let them know I would find the answer they needed and get back to them, and I would always follow through with that promise whether the answer was good or bad. As I began to understand the *hows* and *whys* of our business, I got better at giving immediate feedback. I could explain to the customer the *why* behind how we did business, and they could gain some insight and understanding too. They could learn something, and I learned something in every conversation. I learned where the friction points were between the services we were providing and the customer. This was especially easy to see when the same topics came up repeatedly. These conversations—learning experiences—meant I was not only getting buy-in from my workforce, but I was starting to get buy-in from our customers too.

An example of this comes in the form of an administrative task that everyone in the military has to do periodically: update their ID cards. Although updating your military ID should have been simple, people would get frustrated because of the long lines and wait time involved. This process was managed by a department within the garrison, and the members of that department were clear that the customers were right—wait times were too long.

We listened to the complaints and decided to conduct the process of updating ID cards by appointment. People could go online and make an appointment, and we promised to see them within 15 minutes of their appointment time. All we had to do was meet our promise to the customer, which was made easier by controlling the number of customers waiting at any given time. Our productivity improved, and the customers were happy. Again, it didn't happen overnight, and there were some bumps along the way. We learned that we needed to work harder to get the message out on as many information platforms as we could, so people wouldn't show up expecting to be seen right away without an appointment. We would see them, but only after we had served those customers who had appointments. Once the word got out, we received positive feedback. We had listened to our customers, learned from them, and acted on their suggestions.

It is important to know that this didn't happen because of me. It wasn't the result of any decision I made. It was accomplished at the director level. While I had been leading the garrison, I had also sold the director of this department on my vision for customer service and the idea of listening first. He bought into the concept and began to listen to and learn from his customers—the people renewing their IDs.

The director gave me an information brief, not a decision brief. He had decided to change the way his department provided military ID services, and they were doing it to provide first class customer service so it was good to go in my book.

Again, it wasn't my idea, and I didn't implement it. I was not the problem solver there, which brings up an interesting point.

Most people think leaders need to be problem solvers. I agree that, ultimately, you are accountable for any decision your organization makes. It falls on your shoulders, so you need to be able to solve problems and take responsibility for them. However, I would argue that what you really want is an organization that comes to you with a solution to their problems. Your workforce should be actively engaged in solving the problems within their sphere. When this happens, you know you have buy-in.

The way you handle bad news will also encourage your people to come to you with solutions to problems—*or not*. So, let me ask, do you regularly kill the messenger? Do you fly off the handle and expound on the inadequacies of the person or department that has come to you with bad news or a complication? I'm willing to bet that most of us have worked for this type of leader at one point in our careers. It is never fun to be the bearer of bad news, and it only gets worse when the boss goes off the deep end and starts looking for someone to blame—usually not him. Leaders like this remind me of the phrase, "can't see the forest for the trees." Instead of focusing directly on the problem and the *why* the leader focuses on the *who*. It's uncomfortable for the workforce to approach a leader who wants to put someone's head on the chopping block whenever there is a difficult situation. Although bad news never gets better with time, when the boss behaves like this, the workforce will avoid telling them for as long as they can. In the worst cases, they avoid the problem for so long that, when the leader finally hears about it, it is too late to provide a viable solution and, worse still, the leader wastes time reacting badly to the news.

Of course, there have been times when I received bad news, and I would *really* want to explode, but through experience, I learned it was better to focus on the problem and work with the team to find a solution and that is the same strategy I use today. I follow up with an after-action review, implement the changes, and move on. Ultimately the problem must be corrected, so I focus on it first and work with the team to figure out how to prevent it again in the future.

I have found that if you create an environment of empowerment with the expectation that employees should work through the issues themselves and come up with viable solutions, you will not struggle with team members avoiding problems, or withholding information from you. Then you will be empowered to make adjustments as necessary, and you'll have the time to do it, because you aren't using your precious resources on problems that your workforce can and should handle.

BE HUMBLE

We have talked about the definition of leadership, inspiration, authenticity, and the importance of being the best salesperson in your organization. We have discussed building a foundation of trust and finding ways to communicate your vision to your team, but there is one more element I need to cover, and that is humility. This idea is best summed up by a Rick Warren quote that I love: "Humility is not thinking less of yourself, it's thinking of yourself less."

Understanding your privilege is a great way to foster humility in yourself. What do I mean by this? I have always been taught that the opportunity to lead is a privilege. In the Army, because of the nature of our profession, you usually could lead at each level of command for two to three years before moving elsewhere in the organization. It was never lost on me that I occupied a position that 100 other officers could easily have filled. The title of a commander is just that, a title, and although you occupy that position, you will hand that command over to the next officer in a few years. I always understood that I was a "renter and not an owner" in this position, so I was grateful for the time I had at each command position I was privileged to serve in.

With all that said, I think a lot of the times when leaders or their organizations start to fail, it is because they have forgotten that leadership is a privilege, and they should be grateful for the opportunity to lead. They have forgotten that a leader is there to serve those they lead, not the other way around.

You can find several theories about leadership styles, and all have some value. I firmly reside in the camp that believes a leader should be a servant. I don't know how someone who has led men and women into combat could think any other way or why there should be another way. A leader in combat holds responsibility for the life and death of their people, and that obligation is humbling.

Even more humbling is to watch your subordinates take on a mission, make it their own, and succeed. As a servant leader, you lay the foundation for that success, ensure the preparation is conducted properly, and do everything you can to support a successful mission. Then you must let go and watch it unfold, with your subordinate at the lead. When your team members are successful by their own efforts, it is impressive to see. The team becomes closer than they were when they started the mission, and your subordinate is stronger and more confident than before and has probably gained a great deal of invaluable experience.

It is often scary, and at times you as a leader will want to reach in and take the reins, but resist that urge. Your role is to set your employees up for success, so do everything you can, within your power to ensure that result. Then let go and see what happens. If you have done your job well, you can almost predict what will happen. Your monitoring processes will alert you if the mission starts to go off the rails. Then, and only then, should you step in. It's incredibly rewarding to watch a leader grow in confidence and see a mission that they were in charge of have success.

Let me share an example with you. I was in command of an infantry battalion deployed in combat in one of the most conflict-ridden areas of Baghdad. We had learned that most of the insurgent leadership who caused problems for the population in our area were bouncing back and forth from another part of the city. They were unaware that we were tracking them. I worked with my Iraqi counterpart, a brigadier general in the Iraqi National Police, to plan an operation to cordon off and search a part of our area where we knew some of the insurgent leadership were hiding. We worked on this plan for a few weeks.

During this time, one of my company commanders came to me with an idea to capture any "leakers" that may get through the cordon. His plan was to conduct reconnaissance on a mosque that we knew was supporting a lot of the enemy forces. During the cordon and search operation, he suggested that we watch to see if any of the enemy leadership we were looking for tried to hide there. If that occurred, his company would cordon off the mosque and wait for the insurgents to come outside. If they didn't come out, my Iraqi counterpart would send his forces in to clear them out. It was a great idea, and we built it into our plan.

Through intelligence sources, we learned that the insurgent leaders were back in our area, so we executed our plan. With my forces in support of the Iraqi security forces, we started the cordon and search operation. We conducted a systematic clearing of the area while my company commander and his unit conducted reconnaissance of the mosque.

We'd had some success finding lower level enemy leaders, but the reconnaissance team identified elements of the enemy leadership entering the mosque. The cordon and search operation took several hours, and as we finished and started to roll out, the enemy leadership started to leave the mosque. The company commander who conducted the reconnaissance called us in immediately, and we took down most of the insurgents we were after. I asked my Iraqi counterpart to send his troops into the mosque, and they found other enemy leaders hiding there.

The point here is that, although we found some insurgents through the cordon and search operation, it was my company commander's plan for the mosque that really won the day. Because of the success of his idea, we decimated the insurgent cell we were targeting, and most importantly, one of the most contentious areas in our sector became peaceful again.

Local businesses were able to re-open and we established a functioning local government council. Kids started to play outside in their neighborhoods again. It was a high-water mark for that area that allowed us to turn the tide and begin to rebuild all that was lost after years of sectarian fighting. All I did was allow it to happen. We went through the planning and rehearsals, and I was confident that we would have success with both the cordon and search operation and the mosque reconnaissance. Because of my company commander's plan, the area reaped the benefits of peace, and the people there could begin to rebuild. The experience of seeing my company commander have this success and how that success affected others was humbling.

You can support similar success in your subordinates if you realize that you don't need to have all the answers, nor do you have to make all the decisions. You may want to, but if you also want to train your leaders, increase the velocity of decision-making within your organization, and build a learning and thriving company, then you need to let go and empower the people in your organization. Once you do this, you establish an environment of empowerment and innovation, and as a leader, that is incredibly humbling to watch and be a part of.

A great example of this was when I was in command of the garrison at Fort Hood. I was out one day on what we called a garrison commander's battlefield circulation—visiting folks in my different directorates. I was going from one site to another when an emergency call came through: There was a possible shooter in the emergency room at our hospital. It just so happened that I was near the hospital when I got the call. As I came up to the hospital, I saw our Military Police (MP) and Department of the Army Civilian Police (DACP) rush into the emergency room with no regard for setting up a perimeter or getting a better feel for what was really going on. They just rushed in, and more of them were coming. Almost every available MP was converging on the emergency room. I went nuts. I couldn't believe what they were doing. As an infantryman, you are always taught to set up a perimeter, assess the situation, make a hasty plan, get support lined up, and *then* execute. I started grabbing MPs and telling them to get out on the perimeter and find me the person in charge.

In the end, no shooter was present (it was a training exercise that we had not been informed about), but I took the opportunity to find out why the MPs and DACPs executed the way they did. It didn't feel right, and I was certainly not trained that way. When I got the leaders gathered together in front of the emergency room, I was fit to be tied.

"Why would you rush in like that?" I asked.

I knew they hadn't had a description of the shooter, didn't know if there was more than one shooter, and didn't even know the possible location(s) of the shooter(s).

"What if they had tried to escape or other shooters were coming in support?" I asked.

I started to tell them how I had been trained to execute a checklist in combat when one young sergeant stopped me dead in my tracks.

He said, "Sir, we don't rush in to take out the shooter. We rush into protect the innocent people. We rush in to either draw the shooter to us or get the innocents out of harm's way."

Talk about taking the wind right out of my sails! I had just learned something. Yes, it was in front of a bunch of true heroes, and yes, I felt a little embarrassed, but it was valuable information that I hadn't considered.

And it made perfect sense. *That's what we do for our customers.* We protect them. I immediately recognized as many of the MPs and DACPs as I could with Coins of Excellence— an award we used to recognize exceptional service. I gave out all the coins I had in my pocket and my vehicle. I learned something that day, but even better, I gained a greater appreciation for what our MPs and DACPs did for all of us on post every day. These heroes hadn't hesitated for a moment. It was humbling.

The police officers outside the military are just as heroic. If you see a police officer, shake their hand and thank them for protecting us every day. It can be a thankless job at times, but their mission is to make our communities safe so that all of us can follow our dreams, go to dinner and a movie, or do whatever we want. We can go about our business with the knowledge that our police, firefighters, and other emergency personnel do their very best to keep us safe.

Despite the embarrassment, I felt when the young sergeant educated me, I was grateful for the experience because it humbled me in a moment when I was feeling anything but. When I see leaders run into trouble, it is often because they have lost their humility. They forget that their mission is to serve those they lead, not the other way around. It's a slippery slope when they believe they are the reason for any success their organization has. They start to feel entitled, and they are not. Leaders are allowed to lead and should focus on taking care of their people so their people will take care of the organization.

I think it is important to note than in the 25 years I served in the Army, I rarely ever saw leaders who felt entitled. The Army does its best to weed out those kinds of people, but I think it was also rare because we were taught to be humble from the beginning of our careers. Success is not about individuals, but about the team. That mindset re-aligns people's perspective in the best way, and it was one that was impressed upon me from day one of basic training in an episode I now think of as "The Mattress Incident."

When my fellow soldiers and I showed up for basic training, we didn't know each other with a few exceptions. Our drill sergeant gave us the standard welcome speech: "I hope you gave your soul to the Lord because for the next eight weeks your ass is mine! Understood?"

In unison, we all shouted, "Yes, Drill Sergeant!"

Now, some may take issue with how the Army brings in civilians and turns them into soldiers. Some folks will say that the Army breaks them down to build them back up, but I would argue that there is no greater bonding between men and women than when they must perform under stress (in this case, a lot of stress). The Army doesn't break soldiers down. It exposes them to hardship and shows them a way to be successful during stressful times by teaching them the same core values, how to assemble and disassemble a weapon the same way everyone else does, and how to pack a rucksack in a certain way so they all know where to find supplies from another rucksack in case of an emergency. It forces them to find the personal courage to make it through a challenging confidence course alone and as a team. It even teaches them how to make a bed to standard *quickly*. All this contributes to their eventual success in combat, though from the outside looking in, it might not make a lot of sense.

After the welcome speech, we were told which platoon we would be in (there were three and they broke us up by the first initial of our last names), and which floor our platoon would be sleeping on. The drill sergeants allowed us to grab our gear and head up to our floor where we posted ourselves by our designated bunks. In about 30 minutes, they showed us how to store our gear and make our bunks. Then, off we went to apply what they'd taught us. We had 30 minutes to complete this activity and post ourselves outside in the designated platoon formation area. As we stood outside, the drill sergeants inspected our bunks to make sure they were made correctly. I distinctly remember watching my mattress fly out the third-floor window because I hadn't hit the mark.

There were a lot of mattresses thrown out of windows that day. We picked them up, double-timed up the stairs, watched another demonstration. This time, we were given 15 minutes to redo our beds and hustle downstairs. Sure enough, mattresses went flying out the windows again. We picked them up and brought them back up three flights of stairs to our bunks. This round, they gave us even less time to get them to standard. Only, there were fewer beds to make and those that had figured it out already started to help others. We ran down the stairs, and fewer mattresses came out of the windows. Rinse and repeat. We did this faster and faster until, finally, we had *all* had met the standards. We did it as a team.

At the time, I didn't understand the drill sergeants' intent, and I didn't make the connection until later in my career. Our drill sergeants set the expectation that we would only get through basic training if we worked as a team, just like we would in combat. To this day I can clearly see my mattress flying from the window, and now I recognize it as a learning event. I learned that there is nothing more powerful than a platoon of soldiers working in unison towards a common objective. Although it may be a long stretch from making beds to combat, there is nothing more humbling than seeing your organization work together toward a common objective.

TAKE ACTION

1. Develop a leadership philosophy.

Keep it simple, write it down, share it, and go out and live it.

2. Inspire your workforce.

Find your own inspiration and then provide inspired leadership to your organization.

3. Get out and lead.

- Get out of the office and learn about your workforce. You are the one who sets the environment in your organization. Make sure your team knows how special they are to you.

- Get feedback from your workforce and customers then act on it. If you say you are going to do something, then do it.

- Take on each issue as a learning experience for you and your team. Focus on the problem, then the process, then the people.

4. To lead is a privilege. Remind yourself of this every day.

8

FINAL THOUGHTS ON
THE BUY-IN THEORY

*We get 1,440 minutes in every day, no more, no less.
It is a gift. How are you going to spend
those 1,440 minutes?*

G aining buy-in from an organization is not easy. You, as the leader, must work hard to attain it, and keep it; it is so easy to lose. One misstep and you run the risk of having to rebuild. It is worth pursuing though because once you see the power of buy-in within your organization, leadership becomes fun. You focus on the workforce, and the workforce takes care of the company and makes it successful.

You are the standard bearer; you keep your head above the fray and look out over the horizon. You provide guidance and step away, ready to be awed by the power of an organization that, although its individuals may have separate missions, works in unison to make the company better. You serve those you lead and love those you serve. It isn't easy, but it is fun.

The Army has its own way of getting buy-in from its members, and it starts from day one of basic training as mattresses are thrown from windows. There is a method to the madness and it has worked for over 240 years. That said, I don't recommend you throw your employees' possessions out the office window on their first day with the company. Instead, I recommend you take the basic tenets of the Army's method and adapt them to your environment to achieve buy-in.

It still starts from day one, no matter what your environment. It starts with sponsorship programs and focusing on the employee *and* their family. Remember: You recruit an employee; you retain a family. Start new employees with a sponsor of about the same age, sex, and marital status. Make sure the sponsor is on call for the new employee before and during the first few months of employment. Teach the employee the history of the company, its mission, and why it does what it does. Hold a recognition ceremony that introduces the new employee and their family to the organization. Make it a big deal. These simple acts are the foundation of trust in the organization, and they will have you well on your way to buy-in.

What about you as a leader? Is your philosophy sound? Do you live your philosophy every day? What about your vision for the organization? Is it clear, simple, and known to everyone throughout the organization? Does it get your team engaged in making the company better? Are you out there learning everything there is to know about your organization? Are you asking questions—open-ended questions, not yes or no questions? When problems arise, how do you receive that information? How do you provide feedback or guidance to the workforce? Do you know your workforce? Is it made up of Traditionalists, Baby Boomers, Generation X, Y or Z, or do you have a mix? How do they prefer to communicate? How do you prefer to communicate?

Remember, communication is an exchange between two or more people (although I have been known to have the occasional conversation with myself). You are born with two ears and one mouth, so listen more than you talk. Remember, too, that when you talk, people listen to your words, but they pay far more attention to your deeds. So, figure out ways to get out and demonstrate your beliefs to as many members of your workforce as you can. Use different means to convey your information. My thought on this topic is this: If you use every possible form of communication out there, then you can sleep well knowing you have done your best to get the word out to your workforce. However, I guarantee you will get a few people who say, "I didn't know." It is frustrating, but it's just another opportunity to learn from your workforce and to inform them on how to find out what they need to know. When in doubt, I have always found face-to-face is the best way to get the word out. You gain immediate feedback and can answer any questions that come up.

As part of getting out there and leading, you want your workforce to feel comfortable coming to you with bad news or issues that may arise. Beyond that, you *really* want your workforce to identify problems and either come up with recommendations or, even better, implement solutions. Then the problem becomes an after-thought.

Do you have a plan in place to recognize those individuals who do that, who go above and beyond to make your organization better? You could use cash awards; your staff will never turn that down (at least, I know I wouldn't). But sometimes a simple recognition from you, the leader of the organization, can do wonders for an individual and the entire workforce. As I said earlier, if you take care of your workforce, they are going to take care of the business, so look for ways to invest in your workforce. You can invest in rewards, but also consider professional development, in which you create the opportunity and means for people to move up the ladder if that's the path they want to pursue. Take the time to train and develop your team. As garrison commander, my leadership and I figured out a way to do it internally, but there are plenty of organizations that can help train your team. The bottom line is that you should find ways to take care of your people while they are taking care of the business.

Get inspired by what you do and, more importantly, how you do it. You can look to your organization for inspiration as I did in the Army. Every day I found inspiration somewhere within my organization when I needed it. Be grateful for the team you have and be humbled by the fact that your team allows you to lead them. You should never lose sight of the fact that you hold a lot of trust when you lead.

What inspires me the most is when I remember that we only have 1,440 minutes in a day. You and your workforce choose how you spend those 1,440 minutes. You get to decide what kind of day you are going to have. Not every day feels like a good day, but you can always find some good in each day. If you have ever lost a family member or a friend, remind yourself that they don't have the opportunity to decide how they are going to spend those 1,440 minutes. I know that anyone who has lost a battle buddy, a friend, a subordinate, or a leader in combat can relate to this right away. When it seems as if the weight of the world has descended upon me, I reach to my chest and feel my ID tags to remind me that I have an opportunity that those soldiers don't. It is the opportunity to spend those 1,440 minutes any way I choose. I choose to spend it making my piece of the world a little better than I found it, and I do it through the tips and techniques that I have laid out in this book.

I hope that you will find inspiration within this book as well. An idea or two that you can use to make yourself and your organization better.

With my sincere gratitude for taking the time to read this book, I will leave you with one final question: How are you going to spend your next 1,440 minutes?

ABOUT THE AUTHOR

MATTHEW ELLEDGE is a father, a husband, and a Veteran of the United States Army. With 25 years of military leadership experience, Matt has led organizations from 30 to 5,000 people in and out of combat, and he uses these principles to guide others in creating an environment of buy in with their personnel to achieve incredible success in their business.

For more visit EmbracetheEdge.com

Made in the USA
Columbia, SC
04 June 2021